CARMI'S
LOVE STORY

How Ted and Ruth Ann Made the Word
Marriage, "Extraordinary"

CARMI'S LOVE STORY

How Ted and Ruth Ann Made the Word Marriage, "Extraordinary"

GENE SKIPWORTH

ARPress
ILLUMINATING IDEAS
EMPOWERING VOICES

ARPress
45 Dan Road Suite 5
Canton, MA 02021

Hotline: 1(888) 821-0229
Fax: 1(508) 545-7580

Ordering Information:
Quantity sales. Special discounts are available on quantity purchases by corporations, associations, and others. For details, contact the publisher at the address above.

Printed in the United States of America.

ISBN-13:	Softcover	979-8-89389-278-9
	eBook	979-8-89389-279-6
	Hardback	979-8-89389-280-2

Library of Congress Control Number: 2024908154

TABLE OF CONTENTS

INTRODUCTION

We were at basketball practice after school in the gym at Washington Junior High School in Carmi, Illinois. Preston Cole was the coach, and he had been yelling at Gene Murdock who was playing center. He was the tallest of us eighth graders at 5'10". (In fact, he was the last in line at our eighth-grade graduation, because we were placed in line by height.) Coach Cole was yelling at him to pass off when the guards crisscrossed by his post position as they were breaking for the basket. After he yelled at Gene for the third time, we ran the play again and Gene still did not pass off, but turned and shot a jumper. Coach blew his whistle, and we all got silent knowing what was going to happen.

As we waited for Coach to let Gene have it again, Goob Sexton, one of the guards and one of the school's best athletes, looked at me and nodded up to the highest part of the bleachers. Everyone else turned to look up, even Gene, as the coach was yelling at him. Up high at the farthest distance from the floor was Ted Smith, a sophomore at Carmi Township High School. Even as a sophomore Ted was the star on the high school football team. He was the one guy all of us boys looked up to. He was our hero. He was by far the best athlete in Carmi, maybe ever. (The second best, near Ted Smith, was Ronnie Winter. At the time Ronnie was in the sixth grade but played one of the guards on the junior high basketball team and was probably our best player.)

We all just stared at Ted Smith sitting high up in the bleachers, watching our practice. Goob, LeRoy Miller, Stan Williams, Roger Given, and I had our eyes on Ted Smith. Coach had to blow his whistle a couple of times to get our attention. But there was Ted Smith, up high in the bleachers, eating a large loaf of cinnamon bread and drinking a quart of milk out of the bottle! Man, was he the jock!

He was eating a loaf of cinnamon bread from Wehrley's Confectionary. (In the 40's and 50's most small towns had a "confectionary." That was another name for a place that served fountain drinks, sandwiches, pastries, candies, and served as a drug store and sometimes, a five and dime.) Wehrley's had the best bakery from several miles around. Their large loaf of cinnamon bread was their signature item that really made your mouth water. And there was Ted Smith, high in the bleachers watching us practice, eating his large loaf of cinnamon bread and drinking his quart of milk out of the bottle.

That was Ted Smith. As a senior at Carmi Township High School, he was designated in the 1953 yearbook as "Best All Around." With Ruth Ann Ward by his side, they became "Carmi's Love Story."

Ted and Ruth Ann

CHAPTER I:

"STOP THE GREEN PERFUNCTORY"

It all started in Carmi in 1948. Four sixth graders went to the Carmi Theater for a Saturday afternoon matinee. Four kids, Ruth Ann and Bob, Francis, and Ted were at the Saturday matinee. They probably met at the popcorn machine in the small entryway after they bought their own tickets. Then they got their sack of popcorn and coke and went into the theater and sat down.

Nothing happened during the movie. No holding hands or getting close in the seats. They probably didn't even share the popcorn. After the movie, nothing happened on the walk home, either. Ruth Ann's house was their first stop. When they got to her house, she went up the steps to the screen door of the porch. She and Bob were standing on the top step. But Bob did not make a move toward Ruth Ann. Ted thought, "He is just standing there wasting time. He is just talking. Probably saying nothing. We have to get going." (In seminary, we called that useless verbiage that Bob was giving Ruth Ann, "Green Perfunctory.")

So, Ted, getting impatient for a sixth grader, said, "Hurry up, if you aren't going to kiss her, I will." With that Bob backed off, Ted took his place and kissed Ruth Ann. Bob was speechless and didn't know what to say or do. The three of them walked off to take Francis home.

That was the last time Bob had a "date" with Ruth Ann. That is when THE BEST ALL AROUND took over.

For the next seven years, until 1953, Ted and Ruth Ann spent a lot of time walking home from Ted's sports events, often hand in hand, from the school track, basketball gym, football field, or baseball diamond to Ruth Ann's top step to the screened in front porch. The only difference was that as they entered junior high, Ruth Ann often wore her cheerleader's uniform and saddle shoes.

That Saturday afternoon matinee at the Carmi Theater and the walk home really started something. And "Bob, if you don't kiss her, I will" seemed to be the catalyst that started something no one could imagine happening. Just think, "If you don't kiss her, I will" created a journey for two people for over seventy years and impacted the lives of their parents, created the lives of two wonderful daughters, welcomed the lives of grandchildren and great-grandchildren, touched the lives of nieces, nephews, family, and friends. Could Ted's impetuous "If you don't kiss her, I will" fashion all that has taken place? Could one simple statement be so influential and make such an impact on so many people? Maybe we could start a new phrase called "The Tedsmithism," "BE CAREFUL WHO YOU KISS, SHE MAY STICK WITH YOU THE REST OF YOUR LIFE."

CHAPTER II:

"YOU CAUGHT THEM DOING WHAT?"

In 1953 there were 485 students, teachers, and staff involved at Carmi Township High School. There were 442 students (143 freshmen, 101 sophomores [my class], 132 juniors [Ruth Ann's class], and 66 seniors [Ted's class]). There were 3 janitors, 6 bus drivers, and 3 cooks. CTHS had 20 faculty members, 4 administrators, 5 school board members, and 2 secretaries.

Of the four hundred and eighty-five people who were actively involved at Carmi Township High School, I am the only one who saw it. No one else was close. Where were the four hundred and eighty-four other people? Why did fate single me out as the privileged one? I couldn't believe it! I looked around for somebody to confirm what I had just seen. No one was within shouting distance; I just stood there, watching. I had taken the first step in the north stairwell and looked up and on the first middle-turn of the stairs stood Ted Smith and Ruth Ann Ward.

I couldn't believe what they were doing. Encompassed in all the giggles and muffled laughter, they were exchanging bubble gum! Not unwrapping it and passing it on to the other person with their fingers but passing it back and forth mouth to mouth! **What!** People never kissed in school! And people never did such a thing as this in school either. No wonder Ted Smith and Ruth Ann Ward were alone in the most remote and dark and isolated place in the school building. And I was the only one in four hundred eighty-five people to see it. Who in the world would believe me when I tell them about this? What in the world would I tell them I saw?

Then Ted and Ruth Ann finally looked down (when they bothered to take a break) and saw me, they didn't panic or run away or yell at me. They simply said, with all smiles, "Hi, Skip."

I told my good friend Jack Hill what I saw. Our sophomore minds thought, "We don't know if we would call passing bubble-gum back and forth mouth to mouth as juvenile." That is something a more mature adult would do, not a junior or senior in high school. We can't imagine Ted Smith doing anything juvenile.

I knew and everybody in school knew that Ted Smith and Ruth Ann Ward were a couple. Everybody knew they were dating. But exchanging bubble-gum mouth to mouth? Wait till I tell Goob Sexton about this! He won't believe it. He will tell Roger Given and LeRoy Miller and they will tell Stan Williams. Then they are all going to say, "Skipworth doesn't know what the hell he is talking about."

I was the only one in four hundred and eighty-five people who saw it. The indelible image will always be etched in the eternal annals of the stairwell of Carmi Township High School. But the school burned down a year later, and so that indelible image will no longer be etched in the eternal annals of the stairwell of Carmi Township High School.

Ted was the first high school student in Carmi to wear "wingtip" dress shoes! Several of us were shooting baskets at Johnny Rice's house in the back driveway. Ted walked up and joined us and started shooting and then we all recognized his new "wingtip" dress shoes. And they had the wide souls that stuck out. Everybody told him, "Man, those 'wingtip' shoes are really nice."

Ted Smith also was one of the first guys in Carmi to get a flat top haircut. Carmi had not seen many flat top haircuts, but after Ted Smith got his, we all got one. And, if Ted Smith kept his all through the school year, we all did too. All the guys in my class got a flat top. Some guys looked fantastic in a flat top: flat tops, however, didn't make everybody look good. Some flat tops just didn't do it. Richard Reynolds and Stan Williams were the two most handsome guys in the school, and their flat-tops just didn't do it.

In our 1953 yearbook, the sophomore class pictures had twelve guys with flat tops and some of those twelve had their hair grown back only after Ted Smith graduated.

And Ruth Ann Ward? Man, she made the testosterone level of thirteen-and fourteen-year-old boys jump. As the drum-major she was in front in all the parades and at halftime at the football games, she was the star who performed in front of the band. Her biggest role was captain of the cheerleaders.

CHAPTER III:

WHERE IS CARMI, ILLINOIS?

Carmi, Illinois is the only town in the world where an eighth-grade kid could win a contest sponsored by the city council to design a city park. Everyone was invited to enter the contest. All the citizens of Carmi were invited to submit their plans, their drawings, and creative ideas for the park. Richard Reynolds submitted his plans. He was only an eighth grader but was an excellent artist at his age.

He designed the layout for Eckerly Park. It included a ball diamond, swimming pool, tennis courts, swings and other apparatus, a concession stand, and picnic area with a shelter. All of it was designed by this eighth-grader, not the city engineer, not the county engineer, not a professor of architecture at Evansville College, not the retired construction engineer from Halliburton, not any respected adult in the city, but young Richard Reynolds.

Several people entered and submitted a plan. But the Carmi City Council chose Richard's plans and the park was built and fashioned around those plans. Only in Carmi could such a major decision be made to recognize the contribution of an eight-grade boy.

I got the job of maintaining the park once it was developed. I was hired when I was a sophomore in high school. My boss was Preston

Cole, the gym and industrial education teacher at Washington Junior High School. He was also the junior high basketball coach.

Carmi is known as the *"Watermelon Capital of the World."* (There are also fifteen other towns in southern Illinois designated as the Watermelon Capital of the World.) Carmi was also known as *"The Wabash River Town."* (But there were four other towns along the Wabash River in southern Illinois that were known as **The** Wabash River Town.) Carmi was known as the *"Oil-boom Capital of southern Illinois."* (There were six other towns in White County alone that were known as the Oil-boom Capital of Illinois.) Carmi was known as the *"Corn Day Capital of the Mid-west."* (There are dozens of towns in the mid-west that have a Corn Day.)

For those of us who grew up and went to school in Carmi, one thing about Carmi made it the symbol of what a small town is all about, the phenomenon of Saturday night. Talk about being busy, active, excitement, and special! The three blocks of downtown Carmi were packed with people. The cars were parked on Main Street parallel to the sidewalk and each parking space was filled. As far as one could see down Main Street, there were cars parked on each side of the street. The side streets on either side of the main street were also filled with parked cars. It was that way from about noon until about ten P.M. every Saturday night.

All the stores were open, people were doing their shopping, people were having conversations and sharing news and catching up on what is happening. It was a very special time with a festive atmosphere, a celebratory mood, a time to "reconnect," and revel in being a part of "small-town USA."

Main street on Saturday night had traffic bumper to bumper, car horns blaring when the driver, or passenger, saw a friend. The cars cruised up and down Main Street as a u-turn was made at one end of one "pass" through the main drag then another u-turn at the other end to make another run.

Carmi was and is a small town of fifty-five hundred folk. The Skipworth family moved to Carmi in 1949 and the population signs on the outskirts of town said, "5500." In 2023 the signs still say, "5500."

We moved to Illinois in 1939 because my father was an oilfield worker and southern Illinois was where a major oil boom took place in the mid to late thirties. We lived in Brownstown, St. Elmo, Avena, Norris City, New Haven, and then Carmi where I attended junior high and high school.

The first mile north of Carmi was the location of all the oil field companies, their equipment, supplies, and trucks. I don't remember the number of oil companies which had buildings, offices, and property to hold all the equipment. But the number was exceptional for a small town. One could get an idea of the number of oil companies by the number of giant trucks with their loads of pulling units, rigs, pipelines, and sputters that came through town every day, several times a day.

The coal industry was also a big money-maker for Carmi. I knew very little about the coal business in White County, but it was one of the biggest employers in the county. The mine that gave Carmi the reputation of producing coal, was located on the black-topped road leading to Epworth.

Carmi was the typical small-town USA. It filled all the stereotypical expectations of small-town USA. The old square brick Carnegie library, the typical "confectionary," Western Auto Hardware, grocery stores (individual ownership – like Mattix Grocery, Fairchild Grocery - no super-markets), service gas stations that wiped the windshields, barber shops that sounded like barber shops, hardware stores that sold sporting goods, grocery stores that had only six different breakfast cereals (not the thirty-five choices today), grocery stores that sold milk in glass bottles, doctors who made house calls, and a horse drawn wagon that came around to clean out all the out-houses.

When I was in junior high school and high school, it seems to me that while living in Carmi during the 1950's, everybody went to church. I know the Maunie General Baptist Church, just outside town, near the river, was always full each Sunday. My best friend, Lester Rippy went there and when I went with him, it was full. My own church, Emmanuel Evangelical United Brethren Church, was also always full each Sunday. The balcony would be almost filled. The choir loft was filled. The Sunday School classes were always at capacity. The place to be on Sunday morning? Church.

The same was true for Sunday night services. The church wasn't packed, but there were plenty of people there. And, that includes young people. We wore suits and ties and dress shoes. Two or three car loads of church going youth would leave after Sunday night worship and go to Brown's watermelon patch and "take" two or three watermelons and go to the park and spit out seeds.

Carmi and White County politics were primarily Democratic but within the southern Illinois flavor and conservative side on the issues. There were Republicans who made their presence felt. But the political landscape, regardless of the political party, had its expression and activity influenced by the "Bible-belt" cultural inclination. What church you belonged to was the more dominate question than what political party you belonged to. Where you worked was more important to find out than what political party you belonged to.

What you did or where you went after high school was asked more often than who you voted for. A symbol of the lack of extremist "lightening-rod" political conversation was the popularity of one of the leaders who held public office for many years.

Goob Sexton, a good friend and member of my class of '55, was popular with both political parties. His reputation of being a star athlete at CTHS, a standout football player at Millikin University, and a generous community personality made him loved and respected. He exemplified what Carmi valued; hard work, being a "doer," making a contribution to the town, and making a difference.

In 1953 the elementary, junior high, and high schools were all at capacity, the population of Carmi was not dominated by the elderly or seniors. The oil production companies were a peak operation and needed young able-bodied persons. The businesses downtown were all thriving and looking ahead to continued prosperity. Parents took an active part in the activities of the schools. Sports events were well attended with crowds that were very special spectators. Carmi was a clean town, many said it was "pretty," it was safe and there were no thoughts of having the police patrol the hallways at school (it was the decade of the 50's!), the churches were busy and not one was "hanging on the vine" to die, the streets were free of potholes, downtown stores were solid businesses, there seemed to be an absence of "trouble-makers," and even the "cliques" were healthy and non-obtrusive.

Carmi had another place of designated importance. We lived in that "designated" place. It was "across the tracks." Several families who lived there were families that had their roots, their livelihood, in the oilfields. I hesitate to say the families "across the tracks" were poor. We weren't exactly poor, but living there didn't cause us to think we were well off. In any event, the reference to where we lived usually was etched in the words, "Oh, you live across the tracks."

Growing up in Carmi gave us a small-town mindset. Growing up in Carmi made us naïve about many things, but only because we had very few chances to encounter issues outside Carmi. Simple unassuming folk were content to stay in their own backyard and were suspect of those who wanted to venture in. Although we were inexperienced in some aspects of what was taking place in the world, and even though we were naïve on many issues, Carmi was a great place in which to grow up.

Small town U.S.A. Carmi Bulldogs. Purple and White. Coach McDougal. Coach Shroyer. Coach "Babe" Hillyard. State of Illinois gymnastic champion, Gary Danner. Ted's senior class was 1953 and had 66 graduates. As juniors they had 74 students. They lost 8 students in that one year. Ruth Ann's class was 1954 and had 105 graduates. As juniors they had 132. They lost 27 students! Why? How? Did they drop out or move away? In most small towns in the U.S.A., changes in the population of the schools from the freshman year to the senior year is obvious.

Everyone from Carmi would say that Carmi is not the typical small town. They would say there is something unique about it. For instance, for the first time in US history, a graduating class (the CTHS Class of 1952) had a PRAYER printed in the year book in its first page of introduction. It started out with, *"FOR THIS WE PRAY"* and then the prayer. **"BLESS US, THE SENIORS. MAY WE LIVE LIVES THAT EMULATE THE MASTER. FORGIVE OUR FAULTS, THOUGH THEY BE MANY, AND GUIDE OUR STEPS, OUR MINDS, OUR SOULS TOWARD AN EVER-HIGHER GOAL. MAY WE WHO NOW LEAVE CREATE HOMES WHERE THOU WILL EVER BE, AND MAY ALL OF US – PROTESTANT, CATHOLIC, JEW – COME THROUGH OUR DAILY LIVES, TO PROVE WHAT 'LOVE THY NEIGHBOR' MEANS. FOR THIS WE PRAY."**

The question? Who put the prayer together? What were the circumstances or conversation that got the prayer printed, placed in the 1952 Year Book, and has with- stood these seventy plus years? Such a huge and unique contribution to a high school year book! And, it wasn't a "third-grade theology" that came up with *"May all of us-protestant, catholic, Jew-come through our daily lives, to prove what 'Love thy neighbor' means."*

Where is Carmi, Illinois? Carmi Township High School, is just a few miles west of Maunie in White County, about seven miles south of

Crossville. Main Street in Carmi is on the banks of the Little Wabash River, just a short distance west of the Ohio River, a shorter distance west of the Wabash River, four miles north from Union Ridge, six miles east of Burnt Prairie, just north of Dog Town and twenty miles west of Evansville, Indiana. Carmi is forty miles north of Carbondale, Illinois, almost three hours south of Champaign, seven hours south of Chicago. The cement formed Carmi Bulldog mascot that weighs half a ton, sits in front of the high school, in the southeast corner of the state.

CHAPTER IV:

TWO OVERACHIEVERS

A. Ted – "The Best"

In the Carmi Township High School year book of 1953, Ted Smith was named, confirmed, and officially recognized as the *"BEST ALL AROUND."* It is a good thing that the person or persons who named Ted as *BEST ALL AROUND* never saw him and Ruth Ann in that darkened stairwell. No telling what he might be named. On the other hand, maybe that is why he was named *BEST ALL AROUND*; maybe they did see him and Ruth Ann in that darkened stairwell!

Other students of his class of 1953 were also recognized, but they were just named or recognized as *"Most* Likely to Succeed," *"Most* Intelligent," *"Most* Friendly," but not *"BEST!"* And, if you knew Ted Smith, you knew he was *BEST ALL AROUND*. Most of us sophomore boys knew him as the *BEST* in everything.

But who selected Ted as *"Best All Around?"* Was it a committee of two, or three, or did the chair of the committee select "Best All Around?" Did the faculty decide? Was the school board asked to help in the selection? Whoever named Ted Smith as the "Best All Around" got it right. My friends and I would have voted for him when we saw him in the gym at Washington Junior High during our basketball practice when he was eating that loaf of cinnamon bread and drinking from a whole quart bottle of milk. Talk about a stud!

There were only thirty-six in Ted's graduating class of 1953. Only Ted was selected as "Best" and only six were selected as "Most Likely." Only seven people qualified? Only twenty-five percent of the class made it?

There are pictures of each graduating senior in the yearbook and under each individual picture are the accolades they earned as a student at Carmi Township High School. One student had ten lines of accolades listed; and she didn't get recognized for anything!

One person had these accolades under her name, "Prom attendant," "Homecoming Court," "Class Play," "Class Officer" and was not selected for anything. And "Most intelligent?" The most intelligent in my class of '55 had the best grades, but didn't know who won the '55 World Series!

Another person had accolades that included "Student Council" all four years, "Student Council President," "National Honor Society," "Junior Academy of Science Award," "Citizenship Award," "Science Club," "Hi Tri," "FHA," and she wasn't just "Prom Attendant," she was on the "Prom Committee!" But she just barely made the twenty-five percent.

Ted, like a few kids who grew up in a less favorable environment, was the rare high school student who everybody liked. He had the respect of not only the students, but the faculty as well. Ted was a model student. As well as being respected, he respected others, especially the teachers. He was not a discipline problem in the four years of high school. He was a ready volunteer for those things that had to be done with no accolades to receive. Their daughter Joan says that her dad was a man of few words. She said, "When he did talk, we listened very closely. He never had much to say, but we all listened because it was going to be good. He is the kindest man I have ever known. I am so glad he is my father."

B. Ruth Ann - "Spoiled Rotten Sixteen-Year-Old Girl"

At sixteen years of age, Ruth Ann Ward was a naive, but a beautiful and talented young lady (and as she said so often to her closest friends) "a spoiled rotten 16-year-old girl." She had two older brothers who looked after their little sister and really aided in the spoiling of Ruth Ann.

Now, she is facing a traumatic future with a mountain of uncertainties and anxieties. She did not finish her senior year of high school, which is one of the most important, growing, sharing, experiences one can have with friends. Ruth Ann was no longer at the center in a fun environment in which she thrived as the "most popular" girl. Now she was preparing to take on a more serious role. A role unfamiliar to a "spoiled rotten 16-year-old." She was looking down the road to being a wife and mother.

Ruth Ann stood out as a sixteen-year-old high school junior, cheerleader, and baton twirler going with the number one high school jock (who was voted *"BEST ALL AROUND"*). She had her future in her hands in any dimension she wanted. The prospects ahead were wide-open; any college, and any career path she might choose.

One could expect nothing but the best. Students who were just acquainted with her and her close friends looked upon her as "princess." Although many considered her "above" the rest, she did not practice or behave like she was "above."

One would think that she had lost everything with this new "snag" in her path. But she and Ted never saw the prospects of having a baby being a "snag." What one would call a costly mistake, they saw as a blessing, an early challenge for their young lives together, an opportunity to show their resilience and maturity, and they saw it only as a step into the future sooner than they expected.

Going into the immediate future with the cost of missing her senior year of high school and not having a big wedding, may sound like too big a hurdle for a young sixteen-year-old girl and a seventeen-year-old boy. But not to Ruth Ann and Ted. They were going to make sure their lives would be the beginning of a fulfilling life together, with a beautiful daughter, the wonderful experience of a family fashioned around love, Ted's opportunity to play college football, their desire to succeed in meeting a challenge, and a family bonded as a blessing to enrich their lives.

Ruth Ann had no want for money or things. One would think that Ruth Ann would be undisciplined when it came to money, being she was the self-designated spoiled rotten sixteen-year-old girl. But by her needing to be frugal and wise about money matters, while the family was in the most vulnerable of conditions during the Millikin years, she was the steady force that kept the family comfortable and free of need.

In high school as well as during the Millikin years, Ruth Ann looked like she was modeling for *Teen Magazine.* She was always dressed very well. That may be the logical and "makes sense to me" reason that she gave Jan the middle name of "KORET" which was the name of the famous first-class women's bathing suit at the time from California. She looked like she could be called anytime to do a commercial for the clothes selections at Marshall Field in Chicago or a Prell shampoo ad. Eric, the husband of Jan, has said, "I think she has everything she ever wanted."

Ted and Ruth Ann became one of the most identifiable couples at Carmi Township High School. Oh, people knew about Goob and Joyce, John and Janet, Gary and Neta, Stan and Delores, and many other "couples." But somehow, Ted and Ruth Ann gave the impression that they belonged to each other. They gave the feeling that this was not just a high school couple.

They gave the perception that they were the mature ones at CTHS. As some of their friends describe them, "Everyone respected Ted and Ruth Ann. They were at the very top of the "pecking order" as to who was most reliable, most liked, and most respected. They gave the very healthy impression of being confident. Not aloof or far removed from the mainstream. Their confidence was in who they were and confident in what they were going to accomplish. They were the exception of high school couples who seemed serious about their relationship."

C. Opposites Do Attract

As individuals, Ted and Ruth Ann were different as day and night. They came from families and homes that had few characteristics in common. Their backgrounds were different and their individual personalities different and to think one could put them together seemed insurmountable.

Ted came from the far northside of Carmi on a small farm which was not the most endearing place to live. The Smiths had no running water, an outhouse, and little semblance of a 1950's middle-class home. His family shied away from the limelight, the crowds, and seldom was seen at any of Ted's athletic events. A good way to characterize Ted's background and "place" in the community of Carmi would be to say, "He was from across the tracks."

Jan, the oldest daughter, and Joan, the youngest daughter, said they had spent some very enjoyable visits with Ted's parents on their small farm. There was a stream which ran through their property, there were dairy cows and chickens. Jan said that she and Joan found a large flat rock near the creek on which they would lay down and just take in the sun. One day, one of the cows came up to them and put its face down to Jan's as she was laying on the rock.

Jan said she remembers their grandpa holding a chicken high over his head and wringing its neck. For Jan and Joan, spending time with Ted's parents was a relaxing and enjoyable time. It was one of the most memorable experiences in their young lives to visit their grandparents.

Joan said on one of their visits with Grandpa and Grandma Smith she had her first experience of milking a cow. "Grandpa helped me learn how, but I remember it was hard to do. But with the milk in the bucket, I felt I had accomplished a lot. I felt that way especially when grandpa took my finished 'work' and put it through the milk separator to get it ready to drink."

Joan said, "It was a wonderful experience being with Grandpa and Grandma Smith. It was different being there. We felt they really loved us and enjoyed being around us. Being on that small farm with them was something I just ate up. They were very shy, they didn't say much, and they kept to themselves. But Jan and I felt their love and care for us, and they always made us feel they were glad we were their granddaughters.

Sometimes we would spend the night there. One time I remember we did and Dad and Mom were also there. Dad and Mom slept on the floor and Jan and I shared the bed. It seemed when we all were there at Grandpa and Grandma Smith's, it was a very complete feeling." As time went on and the girls became women and had their own families, the memories of those weekends at Grandpa and Grandma Smith's small farm became more and more of a treasure.

I asked Ted what were the values that he learned from his folks. He never took any time to think of an answer. "Three things come to mind. First of all, my folks had a saying that I have never forgotten; 'One can't always be right, but one can always be honest.' The other thing I learned was from my dad and it was, how to work. He worked two farms of forty acres each. He worked as a dry-waller, an ice house attendant, and he added to that a bunch of side jobs. He really showed us a work ethic that stuck to each of us kids. The third thing he taught us was an example he set; he never let alcohol touch his mouth. Even when we kids got sick with the croup or a bad cough, he wouldn't give us anything that had alcohol. What he did give us was a little sugar mixed with kerosene. I can tell you it worked."

D. 1953 to seventy years later, 2023

It would have been interesting to have an added category to the seniors who were listed in the 1953 yearbook. The added category to the listed seniors in the class of 53, could have been DO YOU REMEMBER? I can see a very interesting series of discussions on the topic. *"Most Likely to Foresee the Future."* It would be interesting to work on a project that would officially list all the devices, concoctions, products, and gadgets that were invented from 1953 to 2023. My bet is that more innovations were developed in **these** past seventy years than any other seventy-year period in history.

Could that person in the class of '53 *(Most Likely to Foresee the future)* do some creative thinking to come up with all the inventions, conveniences, and "stuff" that we now take for granted? I wonder what the high school experience would have been like if we had a CELL PHONE? Could a high school student from Carmi come up with the thought of a COLOR TV? or a SPACE CAPSULE? And could 1953 high school football players ever come up with a WRAP-AROUND-FACEMASK for the football helmet? Could a graduating senior of the class of 1953 from Carmi Township High School believe in the possibility of a man LANDING ON THE MOON? Could we imagine adding something like a MICROWAVE to our kitchen? Could we concoct or imagine something in our minds like a LAPTOP? Or as an athlete, could we concoct or imagine something in our minds like the possibility of a SUB-FOUR-MINUTE MILE? The past seven decades could have an insurmountable list of new creations found in every home.

When we consider seventy years, we cover a lot of years and a lot of life changing experiences. Lives go through multiple changes in seventy years. Lives are touched by tragedy, celebrations, trauma, hope, sadness, job, darkness, light, and a host of life-changing confrontations, challenges, and jobs.

Seventy years, side by side, Ted and Ruth Ann being absorbed by the presence of each other, were touched to the core of the inner-most part of the human soul. One good friend from high school, said seventy years later, "When we talk about Ted and Ruth Ann being together all the time, they not only worked side by side for several years, but they did good work together. They also were best of friends to each other during all that time."

E. My First Encounter with Ted Smith

For those of us who were freshmen or sophomores, Ted Smith was identified with football. He was "all around" in the activities and academics in high school. But, for most of us, he was a football player. During a football practice, I was a reserve halfback and we were practicing with some of the varsity by catching and running punt returns. John Rice was punting and a few of us reserve players would catch the punt and run it back. The varsity was practicing tackling the punt returner. (I was deep in the chart in the "reserves," something like fifteenth on the reserve depth chart of twelve.)

The only problem with the practice of returning punts, was that coming down to practice tackling were the five biggest guys on the team; Paul Mauntel, Joe Dill, Jack Legier, Marion Knox, and Bill Langford. They were not only big, but they were also five of the best players in southern Illinois. (At least they looked that way as I got ready to receive the punt!)

It was my turn to receive the punt. John punted the ball, and all I saw were those five guys coming toward me. I felt they were not coming toward me, but AT me. I didn't pay much attention to the ball. It hit me on the shoulder pads, bounced into the air, I reached for it, missed it again and it rolled away. The five monsters ran past me and returned to their places for another try.

Coach Shroyer yelled from where John punted the ball so everyone could hear what he said, "Skipworth, you are as useless as tits on a bore pig." At my age and inexperience with pigs, I didn't know what that meant. My first encounter with Ted Smith was when I looked to my right and saw him and some of his varsity teammates bending over laughing.

At the Johnson City game, about two weeks later on a Friday night, I encountered Ted Smith the second time. As a reserve deep in the reserve team depth chart, I was put in the game with Johnson City toward the end of the game. Coach Shroyer put me in at defensive halfback. He said it was a position where I couldn't do any damage.

On the next play the ball was given to Jan Jansco, their star running back. In fact, Jansco made All State in Illinois and was given a football scholarship to the University of Illinois. He was coming around their left side, toward me. He was looking at his right, not paying any attention to me as I was coming up on him. I had a clear shot at him. I was thinking how proud Coach Shroyer would be of me and how he would complement me on a great tackle on Jansco. I was also thinking how Ted Smith would see it all and say, "Skipworth, you ought to be on the varsity after what you did to Jansco." About that time, I hit Jansco. He knocked me backwards about twelve feet and went on to score from their twenty-yard line.

As I came off the field with the other defensive players, Coach Shroyer yelled at me again, "Skipworth, you are as useless as tits on a bore pig." When I got to the sideline, I was next to Ted Smith who was getting ready to go into the game. I said to him, "That is twice he has said that to me. What does it mean?" Ted said, "You ain't for shit." Then he ran onto the field.

Ted Smith

CHAPTER V:

THE TASK AHEAD

A. Stage One- Anxious Moments

Ruth Ann began to have some questions. "I was just sixteen and didn't know much about the many different functions and physiological changes of a woman. Having changes in my body was one of those 'mysteries' I was going through. I was just learning what most sixteen-year-old girls should know about their bodies. I didn't know everything, but I knew enough to make me suspicious that something was not right. My mother and I never talked about those kinds of things. I didn't want to go to her with a bunch of questions, especially if something was wrong.

"Instead, I went to my dad's secretary. I had gotten acquainted with her and felt, through conversations we had in years past, I could talk to her. For instance, she was the first one I talked to about having a period. Then when I started having all these changes going on, I went to her again. I never thought I was pregnant. After I talked to Mrs. Endicott and told her that there had been some changes with me, she told me I might be pregnant. I never told anybody I might be pregnant, not even Ted, I needed to find out for certain.

"Dad's secretary suggested that if I was pregnant, I should not tell my mom, and especially don't tell my dad until I knew for sure. But for now, she suggested I go see Dr. Harrell. I didn't see Dr. Harrell right away. In fact, I didn't talk to anybody. I didn't even tell my best friend, Nancy.

"Dr. Harrell confirmed the suspicion. When I felt it was the right time, I finally told my mom. But that was a long time coming. I just never wanted to tell my parents because I knew they would really be disappointed. They may have suspected it all along, but they maneuvered around it in such a way that, 'If we don't acknowledge it, maybe it will go away.'

"Eventually it became known among my mom's circle of friends. The terrible result was that her friends would not talk to her. Her best friends literally shunned her. These were good friends that Mom saw often. They were always doing something together. They were friends we went to church with. Good church folk. It was very hard and very perplexing to a young lady who grew up in the church to hear of this response to her mother from her church friends. Where was the grace, the compassion, and the embodiment of Jesus' love? I worried about my mother. Jan suggested that we have to conclude that response was strictly "Bible-belt mentality."

"My mom's friends certainly looked at me differently. All of a sudden, I was no longer the bright talented young lady who had so much going for her. I was no longer the model for other young ladies to follow. They treated my mother the same way. A baby shower for "the girl next door?" No way!

"After a while, I finally told Ted. He couldn't believe it. But it didn't take long for us to decide what we should do. He said, 'This doesn't change anything about the way I feel about you. We are going to get married just as we had planned. We are going to have the baby. We are going to raise that baby with love and affection. Abortion is not an option'."

Ted continued, "We will do what any couple would do who are in love with each other. We will do exactly what we had planned to

24

do. We will get married, I will try to play football for one of the schools that recruited me, I will be a student-athlete, and you and I will both take on the role of father/mother and take care of the baby. That is exactly what we planned anyhow." And they did exactly as they planned. That was what they said seventy years ago! Seventy years of marriage.

"Not many people suspected I was pregnant, just the few I had mentioned it to. As time went on, I didn't get very big. One couldn't tell I was pregnant. I didn't wear maternity clothes. Although my mom made me a nice maternity outfit I did wear on occasion. I wore jeans a lot and I used big baby pins to pin to the waist of the jeans as I got bigger. When the pants got smaller and smaller around my waist, I worked out a system in using the pins so I wouldn't show."

One of the big changes that took place in 1953 was that Ruth Ann didn't attend her senior year of high school. There have been progressive changes in public schools regarding pregnant girls since the 1950's. In the mid-fifties, very few public high school students could attend if she was pregnant. In 1953, the local school boards became stricter with the individual student. Many of the agendas of local school board meetings included time for an evaluation of the image of the student body.

In 1953, public education was very different in many ways compared to 2023. Policies, procedures, expectations, and how society determined what was acceptable, all were factors in determining what Ted and Ruth Ann would do in the next few months. There was a period after WWII that female teachers were expected to be single. Married female teachers had the propensity of having babies. When that happened, and they assumed their role as teacher while pregnant, it created a "whispering-stir" among the students and community. Pregnant teachers were just not accepted as a consistent presence in the classrooms and hallways of our public schools.

School districts in the 50's had a much different outlook on sex education, talking about sex, or understanding about sexual orientation. The school board in Carmi, in 1953, determined that pregnant students were often encouraged not to attend school as that would be a sign of the quality of morals and ethical behavior of not only the students but the community. When a female student became pregnant, that became a closed case, and the student began to take a low profile and seldom made their presence known in that community.

In the case of Ruth Ann Ward, she and Ted got married the morning after her Junior Class Prom on Saturday, May 2. Ruth Ann was not seen much that summer of 1953, did not attend Carmi Township High School her senior year, made very few public appearances, and turned seventeen. Shortly after Jan's birth, Ruth Ann, who had spent months preparing for the day she would become a mother, immediately began to lay out plans for baby formulas, baby clothes, convenience of where to put the diapers, and having her room complete with all the appointments for a good start.

Twenty years later, title IX was designed and provided legislative protection to the pregnant student from discrimination at school. Title IX is a federal civil rights law that protects discrimination on the basis of sex, including pregnancy and parental status in educational programs and activities. The student must be allowed to continue attending school for as long as she wants, even up to the date of her delivery.

B. Stage Two – Young Couple Faces the Challenge

The panic a young couple experiences in similar circumstances is, "What will we do now?" As soon as Ruth Ann told Ted she might be pregnant, Ted made it perfectly clear what they would do. There was no hesitation in his resolve, as he said before, "We will put in place what we have planned. We will get married; I will try to get that football scholarship, and we will go on with our lives. This is exactly what we had planned anyhow. The downtown quarterbacks can spread all the speculation and rumors they want. The truth is, we planned to get married and we will.

"The answer to 'What will we do now?' became clearer the more we talked. The answer has to do with what we want our lives to reflect to the skeptics. We want to show people that we are responsible young people. We are mature and will make mature responsible decisions. Our lives will reflect that maturity and the next few years will show we made good responsible decisions." Ted spoke with the same resolve when he said, "The pregnancy is simply an interruption. We are going on with our plans that we have talked about for months. We love each other, and we are going to get married. We are going on with our plans."

"As I entered my senior year in high school and began my last year playing football, I had been offered football scholarships from six different schools; Nebraska, Murry State, Southern Illinois, Iowa State, Evansville College, and, of all places, New Hampshire. Although I wanted to continue playing football and go on to college, another option, but not our first, was that Ruth Ann and I would get married and I would just get a job around Carmi and start working. I didn't really think seriously about college. But, when Ruth Ann told me she was pregnant, that made us stop and think about our future. What would be best for us as a family? We began to consider our best options.

"In June of '53 I went to see Don Shroyer, my high school football coach, to talk to him about college and the scholarship offers I had received. He told me it was too late now to accept those that were offered to me. But he told me that he could get me in at Millikin. So, I began to consider the possibility of attending Millikin and play football. I really wanted to continue playing football, and I wanted to go to college and have Ruth Ann and the baby with me. Ruth Ann wanted the same thing. Because of Ruth Ann's encouragement and support, we planned for this new and exciting dimension to our lives.

"The coach at Millikin, Jack Allen, told me he would give me a scholarship on the basis of what Coach Shroyer told him, but I would have to take the entrance exam. Ruth Ann and I went to Decatur to get acquainted with the coach and make arrangements to take the entrance exam. After taking the exam Ruth Ann and I went to see the coach before we left Decatur. He asked me how I did. I told him I think I did alright. He said, 'You did just fine. You passed with flying colors.' He took care of that."

Most couples going through the experience of an unexpected pregnancy, look with anxiety at the problems they might face. Talk about "lighting-rod" news! Oh yea, "we went to the prom." But how many couples in these fifty states get married the morning after the prom? How many seventeen and eighteen-year-old high school couples take on the role of parents? How many teenagers face the challenge of making major decisions for and with a spouse and for a baby? How many teen aged married couples take on parenting, college, and the truck load of decisions that await them? And, how many do it successfully?

What was behind the success of the marriage of Ted and Ruth Ann? There will be short but affirming statements throughout this book that answer that question. All are true. All fit Ted and Ruth Ann. The answers are varied, but they all add credibility to the success of their seventy years together. Their daughter Jan adds this one very important factor, "They had a *United Front.* And that came about because they *communicated well.*"

Jan interjects this very important thought, "They had success in their marriage because they left Carmi. When they arrived at Millikin, they knew no one. It was unfamiliar in many ways to them. They were young, inexperienced, and lost. The only thing they had was each other. They were close and dependent on each other. This factor was so important in their successful marriage."

They first set out to discuss and work on the decisions to be made, plans to work on, and first steps they should take. They had an idea of what they might face, now it was a matter of how best to handle all those challenges. The questions had a hint of panic in them, especially for a teenage couple. "Will we have enough resources to help in a significant way? How much can we depend on our parents? How much will the comments, rumors, and gossip affect us? Who will stand by us?"

C. Stage Three - Getting Married

Ruth Ann and Ted began to discuss their plans for the wedding. The first thing that Ruth Ann brought up was what kind of wedding it would be. Ruth Ann expressed the feeling that no way did she want a big wedding. Ted was in agreement. The second issue in their planning for the wedding, was to call their former minister at the First Baptist Church in Carmi, Chuck Morris, who they knew. Rev. Morris baptized Ted and Ruth Ann and he was close friends to Ruth Ann's parents. He was now serving the Metropolis Baptist Church, about a two-hour drive from Carmi.

Ted told him of their plans and that they would like to come to Metropolis and be married by him. He told Rev. Morris that they were going to the prom the night of the first of May and wanted to find out if they could get married about mid-morning on Saturday, the 2nd, the day after the prom.

Rev. Morris was surprised but very welcoming to this news that involved two of his favorite young people. They set the time for the ceremony for about 10:00 AM the day after the prom, after all the post-prom parties, and the drive to Metropolis.

Such circumstances present all kinds of questions. Questions of propriety and questions of appropriateness are on the front burner of such an occasion. This young couple going on a two-hour drive to get married? On a Saturday morning and not a community/family occasion at their local church? After their prom? No letters of recommendation or permission? No month-long pastoral pre-marital counseling planning or preparation for such a life-changing event? No legal blood test results initialed by the local county registrar? No mention of the ring purchase or engagement protocol? Just like that, they made the phone call, set the date and time, and when to arrive. Parents, family, friends?

Ruth Ann said she told her mother and she wasn't upset. She said her mother's response was more like being speechless. She said her mom told her dad and no serious repercussions took place. She said her dad took the position that "maybe if I don't talk about it or think about it, it will all go away." Ted did not tell his parents of their plans.

On their way to Metropolis, they did not feel they were "escaping" from the "authorities" nor did they feel they were on the "lam" from the law. They had made their plans which were well thought out, they had touched all the bases and made all the contacts they needed, and they were confident in looking ahead as two persons making responsible decisions.

At each of the post prom parties that Ted and Ruth Ann attended, someone would ask, "When are you two getting married?" Ruth Ann would tell them "After we leave here, we are going to Metropolis and have Rev. Morris marry us." "Oh yea, my foot. You would never do a thing like that. Come on, tell us the truth."

"The last post-prom party we went to was at the home of my good friend Barbara Englebright. After a couple of hours celebrating, we all sat down for breakfast. As we all took our places, for many of us, we realized it would be the last time to gather as class mates. As we took our places, and began eating, Barbara asked, for all to hear, 'Ruth Ann, when are you and Ted going to get married? Everybody here wants to know.' Ruth Ann replied, loud enough for everyone to hear, "We are going to get married in a few hours in Metropolis by Rev. Morris. Everybody there started laughing and making all kinds of cat-calls. Barbara spoke up for everyone there, 'Come on, let us in on your secret of what your plans are.'

"I told Ted, 'As soon as you finish your coffee, let's get the hell out of here.'"

When they arrived in Metropolis, Ruth Ann had changed out of her formal that she wore to the prom. It now was midmorning, and they went directly to the church parsonage, the home of Rev. Morris and his family. Ruth Ann said she was nervous but not afraid or having second thoughts. The nervousness was more a realization that after all the conversations, planning, and anxiety, the time had finally come. Several times on the way down to Metropolis, Ruth Ann had Ted stop so she could puke. She continued the same on the way back after the wedding ceremony.

When they got to the parsonage, they were warmly welcomed by Rev, Morris and his wife Erica. After the pleasantries were exchanged, Rev. Morris asked, "Do you have the license? Ted got the license out of his pocket and handed it to him. Then the Rev. asked who they brought to witness the ceremony and stand with them. Ted said he didn't know they had to have someone. The minister said that was no problem, he would call his neighbor to come over and serve as witness. Not only did the neighbor come over to be a part of the wedding, but her husband came also.

Just a few minutes after 10 A.M. Rev. Morris began the service; a greeting was offered, words of affirmation and blessing were given, the declaration of intention was pronounced, the vows were exchanged, and the ritual of the ring was initiated. Then Rev. Morris made the pronouncement of Mr. and Mrs. Theodore Smith.

In the midst of a glad and joyful spirit at the conclusion of a very meaningful and significant moment, Ted and Ruth Ann saw a "green-light," a clear and unhindered path for their lives together. Now, they had their lives before them. So many challenges and experiences await them.

On their way home they began to talk about their new life together and all the many aspects and discoveries they would be having. As they talked more of their personal preferences and likes and dislikes, they did indeed discover some things about each other they were not aware of. Nothing alarming or anything to put a damper on their celebratory event that just happened at Rev. Morris's home, but a surprise (or shock) to Ruth Ann.

As they were talking about the more personal things like the bed, questions were raised about bed fixtures like pillows: "do you like fluffy pillows, white sheets, colored sheets, heavy blankets, light blankets, a window open, a radio on, a small light on, dark room?" And then they came to "what do you wear to bed?" Ted said "Nothing."

Immediately, Ruth Ann yelled, "Stop the damn car! No pajamas? If you think I am going to put up with that, forget it. Harrisburg is just up the road. We are going to stop at the first department store and we are going in to get you some pajamas. If you don't have pajamas on, don't expect me to get in that bed. What the hell were you thinking?" When they arrived in Harrisburg, they went to the first general store they saw and went in and got Ted some pajamas. And then, they lived happily ever after.

When they returned to Carmi, Ruth Ann didn't go back to her parents' house, and neither did Ted. They went straight to their freshly painted tiny house and quietly started their lives together as a married couple. After all the talking, fantasizing, and teenage dreaming about being married, they were now going to experience firsthand their first attempt, their first trial run at being a married couple. They had this small but very efficient "starter" house. Ruth Ann thought she would start them off in a way that showed maturity, street smarts, what it is to be savvy, and get a jump on being the all-knowing housewife. She would paint the bathroom and not only surprise Ted, but start off their life together by having his accolades beam down upon her.

She found some paint in her parent's garage. Just what she needed for the bathroom project! While Ted was working at his summer job, Ruth Ann painted their bathroom that morning. When Ted got home, the paint was still wet. It hadn't shown any sign of getting dry all day. He saw the can of paint left over near the front door. It turned out to be outdoor all-weather paint. It would have taken two days to dry if used outside. If used on an indoor bathroom, figure on two months to get dry. But Ted praised her maturity, street smarts, savvy, and being all-knowing.

In Carmi rumors did abound. Ted made it known that, "There are only three rumors that matter, and each one is true. *One is the rumor* I will be going on to Millikin to play football and arrive early to participate in fall football practice. That rumor is true. Everything is in place for the care for and attention to Ruth Ann. The preparation amidst the anticipation of the baby being born and the plans made afterward of moving to Decatur are all in place. *The second rumor* is that Ruth Ann will join me as soon as we can get her and the baby ready for the move. That rumor is true. The plans for the move to Decatur have been made and the preparations for the three Smiths are taken care of. Then we will all be in Decatur doing what we had planned all along. *The third rumor* is that Ruth Ann spends most of her day puking which has been taking place over the past three-months. That rumor is true, also."

CHAPTER VI:

THE FIRST ADDITION

A. Jan Makes Three

Jan was born at 2:42 Saturday morning on October 17th at the Carmi Hospital. Ruth Ann said, "I was told by Dr. Strickland that the baby would not be born for at least a couple of weeks. So, on Friday night, my mom and I went to the high school football game. We wanted to get good seats in the bleachers, so at half-time we could see and hear the band perform and the majorettes do their routines. It was also the section of the stands where the cheerleaders led the crowd. Since I was once the lead majorette and lead cheerleader, it was a spot familiar to us all. The only difference was, this time I was sitting in the bleachers and the constant bouncing of the bleachers began to give me the feeling that I was going to be sick.

"During the game I did get sick. As time went on, I got sicker and sicker. Mom and I left the game early because I was feeling terrible. When we got home, I started vomiting. Mom and Dad stayed with me for a while and then decided to take me to the hospital. I was hoping to just go in and find out why I was getting so sick and then get a pill and have it taken care of.

Bea Arbaugh was the nurse on duty and we were acquaintances through both our moms. I told her how sick I had been that evening. She did a quick examination and said, 'You are not sick, you are going to have a baby!' "But Doctor Strickland told me that it would not be for a week or two." 'I am going to call him, because the baby is going to be born now!'

She called Dr. Strickland to tell him to come to the hospital right away, "Ruth Ann is having her baby!" He said, "She is not going to have the baby. She is just acting like a baby. She is getting excited over nothing.' With that word from the Doctor, Bea shouted before she hung up, "Baby Nothing is being born now, as we speak." She took matters into her own hands and delivered Jan into this world. At 2:42 A.M. Jan Koret Smith became a part of the Smith family.

Later that afternoon, Ted was going through the pre-game-warmups for the football game with North Central College in Naperville, Illinois. When the team gathered in the locker room for the last-minute pregame talk, a telegram was delivered to the Millikin dressing room. The telegram was given to the coach, he opened it and started reading. Soon a smile appeared on his face and he said, "This is for Ted. Here, Ted, you read it." Ted told the coach, "I have no secrets, go ahead and read it." The coach started reading it, "This is to inform you that Jan Smith was born at 2:42 A.M. Mother and baby are doing fine." The players all gave Ted pats on the back and they broke out with applause and many yells of "Congratulations." Ted walked over to an isolated place among the lockers and slowly collapsed against the lockers.

Everybody was finishing putting on their uniforms. Ted was attempting to put on his uniform, but things weren't going on as usual. He seemed to be in a daze. Then, a stadium staff member came in and signaled for them to take the field.

As they were leaving the dressing room to go onto the field, Ted was lining up to go out with his teammates. The coach grabbed his arm and said, "Where are you going?" Ted answered, "I am going out with the team." "Do you think you are ready? You only have one sock on. It looks like your shoulder pads are even on backwards.

And, are those the pants to your uniform? I don't think you are ready for this. Why don't you sit down for a while and let this idea of being a father settle in. You don't even have your helmet. You don't even have your cleats on.

"First, I want to tell you something. This is not just another game for you. I want you to listen to me. If we win the toss, we are going to receive. But I don't want you in there until you have a chance to digest this big news you've received. You are excited and nervous. I want you to wait for about the third series of downs before you go in. I want you to have the game in your head, not thinking about the fact of being a father."

North Central won the game, but they didn't have their star player being absorbed by the news he was a father!

After the game, the Millikin team took the team bus back to Decatur. After the bus arrived in Decatur and unloaded the players, Ted quickly got in his car and started the three-and-a-half-hour drive to Carmi. This was an eighteen-year-old NEW father, driving over three hours to meet, see, touch, and experience a new born baby. What could be the effect of these myriad thoughts that weighed heavily on the mind of this eighteen-year-old kid? What range of emotions would he feel in that three-and-a-half-hour drive? **This new born baby was HIS!**

There was no cell phone to use to call someone to help him sort out all those thoughts and emotions he was going through. There was no one in the car for him to raise all the questions that went through his mind, and there were lots of questions. Who is there with Ruth Ann? What was the conversation like around her bed as she is holding the baby in her arms? Was everyone happy? Or, were people weighed down with worry and anxiety? Two teenage kids facing the future with a baby? They don't even have a home, a job, an address, a history, they hardly know each other.

Ted continued to imagine what he would experience when he got to Carmi. "Surely, they would not be angry at me for not being there. The last word from Ruth Ann was that the doctor said the baby would not be born for possibly another week. She told me to go on to the game. Would her parents be upset with me? What will she say to me when I walk into her room? Will she be excited to see me and excited to tell me right away, 'Ted, you won't believe what a wonderful and beautiful daughter we have!'

As Ted put more miles behind him on the way to Carmi, he continued to encounter all kinds of emotions. "I am eighteen years old and I am on my way to meet my daughter. Who can tell me I am ready for this? Who can guarantee that I will be a good father? What can I say that will make me sound like I know what I am doing? How can I put on a convincing show that I am confident in this new role of being a father? I am not convinced I know how to be a good husband. How do I act like I know what I am doing when I am scared to death? How can I assure Ruth Ann that we are going to make it just fine in a new place, a new home, new surroundings, and a new born baby? One thing I am sure of, I have all the confidence in the world in Ruth Ann. And I need not fret, because Ruth Ann has all the confidence in herself.

"When I arrived late Saturday night, after playing in a football game, after a long bus ride back to Millikin, and after quickly getting in my car to drive three-and-a-half-hours, I walked in to the hospital room to see Ruth Ann and Jan. When I walked in the hospital room, Ruth Ann said, in her typical factious sense of humor, 'Ted Smith, where in the hell have you been?' Then with a big broad smile said, 'Did you come to see your beautiful daughter? She is the most beautiful baby girl ever born at Carmi Hospital. Come here! Hold me and kiss me and then you can hold and kiss your daughter'."

Now, with a baby, really important and smart decisions will have to be made in the Smith household. The important point that Ted and

Ruth Ann had talked about for several weeks, was that as time went on, the process of their decision making was that there would be one decision from two people. "Together we will make the decisions on what we do." Big decisions, major decisions, life changing decisions made in a fashion that carried a "mutual" label. One of Ted's teammates expressed words that said it best, "They want what is best for each other."

B. Carry On At Millikin

There was no strung-out planning or struggling such as "Let's think about it." It was as if Ted or Ruth Ann had this all thought through. It was if they had this spontaneous feeling of knowing what to do. The ironic thing about it was that somehow, with Ted and Ruth Ann, the other person "caught" the other person's drift. It was as if the other person was on the same wave-length. Is this trait one of the reasons a relationship lasts for seventy years? Does longevity in a relationship have durability and a lasting effect, due to a mutual but mental "feel" that the couple has for each other?

They had already answered the key question, "What will we do now?" They had decided at the very beginning, "We will carry on as we planned." That was the mantra of this seventeen-year-old mother and eighteen-year-old father. Millikin, football, college student, raising a baby, assuming family responsibilities, taking care of each other, and loving each other with a deep and abiding love; that was the agenda. They never failed to lift each other up.

The more they thought about it, Ted and Ruth Ann broke the answer to the question of "What will we do now?" into three parts. "*The first part of the answer* is an affirmation of our love for each other. There will be no question on what we will do now. We will show everyone what our relationship is like. Our relationship and our future are based on the love that we share. *The second part of the answer* to the question 'What will we do now?' becomes our statement of what we want our lives to reflect to the skeptics. We want to show people that we are responsible young people. We are mature and will make mature responsible decisions. Our lives will reflect that maturity and the next few years will show we made good responsible decisions. *The third part of the answer* to the question, 'What will we do now?' is that we have a vision for ourselves, a vision of success. Our lives, our work, our accomplishments, our role as parents, our love for each other will make that vision come true."

C. Confidence and Trust

Somehow, this young family, laid a solid foundation to fashion the home, the family, the relationship that would last for seventy-plus years. Maybe "last" is not the right word. Maybe the word should be "grow" or "become." As Jan had mentioned in an earlier conversation, "Mom and Dad's relationship is best described as a 'covenant.'"

What was the inner-power or the essence of Ted and Ruth Ann's covenant that made it work? After hearing their verbal expressions of their journey, seeing the visuals they shared, and feeling the experiences so profoundly, two words define and give meaning to that inner strength – *confidence and trust.*

The one place that was a glitch, or the one mark which did not contribute to Ruth Ann's progress, was that she did not finish high school. Ruth Ann's best friends were all very sad that they did not have their good friend Ruth Ann to join them in the last year of high school in Carmi. They had been together as best friends all through grade school. They had experienced many things together. They were supportive to each other when there was a need. When they needed encouragement, they made their presence known; the touch was to give them a feeling of presence, the voice to let them know they weren't alone, the look to let them know they would never be forgotten. They were all sad that Ruth Ann would not be the energy, the up-lifting arm, the hand which always offered help. There would be that emptiness without her.

Did Ruth Ann resent or feel disappointed that her best friends were off to college and she never finished high school? She never expressed that to anybody, especially Ted. With her close friends off to four different colleges experiencing the freedom of a college student, Ruth Ann was changing diapers and awaiting a second baby. But envy was not in her vocabulary. *Confidence and trust* were those factors that enabled Ted and Ruth Ann to fashion a home in love.

Jan said that her mother seldom mentioned that she didn't graduate from high school. "When the subject did come up, she instead began to talk about the family and all that the family has meant to her. She told us in so many ways, she was never sorry about not finishing high school. She always mentioned the alternative, the life she is living, which has proven so much better. She said in some circles she might feel embarrassed about it, but she has always had a very positive attitude about it. There was always the hypothetical alternative by saying, 'Do I want to exchange Jan and the wonderful life we have shared as a family, for a high school diploma?'"

Although Ruth Ann and Ted were very inexperienced in the responsibilities and expectations of a married couple with babies, Ted had a way of coming up with a plan, an answer to the issues they faced. And Ruth Ann spoke and made decisions as though she not only had the knowledge of what to do, but the confidence. For example, when they faced a perplexing problem, one of them would offer, "On the other hand" and then make their comment. It seemed one of them could feel confident that one of them was always thinking ahead.

The issue of not receiving her high school diploma was met with "Yes, but……." Ruth Ann wanted to let everyone know that there were always other ways to having a fulfilling future. Some raised the issue, "But Ruth Ann didn't finish high school. What is she going to do?" When there were moments they felt they were behind the eight-ball, Ted and Ruth Ann had the capacity to think beyond the "wall" that appeared before them. It was the *confidence and trust* that distinguished them from teenagers who were bewildered. Ted and Ruth Ann were teenagers with a sense of direction.

"Almost every day Ruth Ann and I would have three or four of my teammates or fraternity brothers come to our apartment to just hang out. It always was a real pleasure to have them knock on the door and ask if they could come in. Sometimes they would bring treats and sometimes they would bring gifts to the girls. They always brought something over to eat. When we would have these experiences of fraternity brothers or teammates coming over, it seemed to always be a big emotional rush which always gave us a boost. Our personal circumstances may have looked like we are behind the eight-ball but we had so many friends and relationships that gave us so much support and encouragement."

"My teammates knew I didn't drink or party around. They knew I didn't identify with the student whose behavior was free-wheeling and undisciplined. And, when they came to the apartment to spend some time, they knew we were a family with family responsibilities and they conducted themselves by respecting our home and family. It was always a pleasure for us to have them come over. They treated Ruth Ann and me as old friends, but they also were very much aware we were parents. I think that was very intriguing to them. They really liked to tease the girls and make them laugh. In many cases, Ruth Ann and I were younger than most of the players. But since we were parents, that made us the "elderly" and I was the patriarch."

What was being realized in a very significant way, was Ted and Ruth Ann appreciating the life they had. They were making a joyful adjustment to their lives as teenage parents, a married couple living on a college campus, adjustments on the new roles of being husband and wife earlier than planned, and feeling a sense of completeness as they were surrounded by love.

Back home in Carmi, classmates of Ted and Ruth Ann and a few others acquainted with the circumstances raised the big question about the marriage. So many of their friends in the class of '53 expressed the notion so familiar to teenage marriages, "Don't they have too many strikes against them to make it work out?"

The statistics on young teenage marriages are not good as indicators of solid marriages. The strikes against teenagers who "have to get married" have been identified by young couples over several generations. According to two websites regarding teen marriages, the strikes against them become compounded and more obvious as the days and months go by. Divorce in the US is the sixth highest of any country in the world. One website describes this issue with these statements; there is a divorce every 42 seconds. 86 divorces in one hour. 2,046 divorces in one day. 14,364 in one week. High school sweethearts that get married have a divorce rate of 61%. *Another reporter says that 71% of high school sweethearts who have to get married end up in divorce.* The point is that Ted and Ruth Ann face a big challenge.

Consider the following which are obvious strikes against them from the very beginning.

1. **A seventeen-year-old mother? An eighteen-year-old father**? It is difficult for a couple in their twenties or thirties to raise a baby for the first time. Ted and Ruth Ann had **two** babies as teenage parents to care for! In almost any area of a young married couples life's experiences, they did not have the experience or knowledge to deal with them, let alone raising two babies.

2. They both came from **different backgrounds, different families, and different homes**. To make it even more an issue, consider the uniqueness of Ruth Ann, not only being the youngest of three siblings, but the other two were older brothers who catered to their younger sister. That put Ruth Ann in a very unique situation of being the younger sister being attended to by two older brothers as

well as doting parents. She often referred to herself as "a sixteen-year-old spoiled rotten girl." Now, she has taken on the role of mother and wife at age 17. That will take a major adjustment!

3. Being in Decatur and on the campus of Millikin University they were **far from home**. They were far from family, friends and relatives. If they needed help, immediate or not, they had no one to turn to who was familiar to them. They were by themselves. Alone.

4. They were very **inexperienced in the tasks of taking care of a family and home**. They never had to watch the family budget or consider disciplined spending. Now that responsibility was placed directly in their laps. To make it more challenging, they had no resources to give them a cushion to fall back on or get some relief. Ted had more than one job as a student at Millikin, but they were a family of four and they had a tight budget.

5. Ruth Ann was not an introvert! Ted was not an extrovert! **They were different,** but those who knew them then, and even today, say they are inseparable. The old cliché is true in this case, "Opposites are attracted to each other." In so many instances, Ted and Ruth Ann spoke of their decision making as being one voice. They spoke of decisions being made between them as thoughtful and not insisting on their own way. The measure of Ted and Ruth Ann as mature responsible individuals was and is very evident in their seventy years of marriage and the relationship they have with Jan and Joan and family and friends.

6. Six factors make another reason for young couples to have strikes against them. In each example, a young couple seldom has the experience or maturity to overcome these obstacles. The six are; **little attention paid to the other, jealousy, sex, money, housework, control. But somehow, Ted and Ruth Ann had that something inside that rose above those six factors. Confidence and trust?**

7. Probably the biggest reason for all the strikes against young couples that have to get married, is that they have entered into this relationship with **a limited amount of commitment....to each other...to the future...to the challenges ahead...to the marriage.** Couples who are older have a tendency to work out these varied problems. Maturity seems to lend a hand of trying to make things work out. Ted and Ruth Ann never entered into this relationship or marriage with a "limited amount of commitment." They spoke often of a "resolve," a firm unwavering support of each other.

8. Ted and Ruth Ann were asked, "What do *you two* consider the strikes against you?" Ted answered, **"The rumors could have been a real problem. The rumors flew like crazy about us.** Many said that it wouldn't last. They said this is just another teenage marriage that won't last six months. The betting was that our marriage was finished before it started. But *the way we handled the rumors* and all the negative expectations, was to make our resolve even more important."

Something made it happen. Something inside Ted and Ruth Ann embraced them in such a way that their decisions and lives reflected that they had a solid relationship and marriage, in spite of the strikes against them. They met the challenges and they raised a family that demonstrates the power and joy of love which overcame the strikes against them.

What was that "something," the essence, the innate quality inside Ted and Ruth Ann that enabled them to live above the challenges, the "strikes against them?" Birds don't need to be taught to fly. Bears don't need to learn how to hibernate. Ducks don't need to have lessons on how to swim. It is something inside, an innate quality, inherent within a person that compels them to do right and good.

That is what was the source, that something in this relationship with Ted and Ruth Ann; **right and good.**

One of Ruth Ann's closet friends said that "something, that innate quality inside" was expressed in three ways that she observed. First, Ted and Ruth Ann were always looking out for each other. Secondly, they always seemed to be on the same page. And thirdly, they did something that made their relationship unique, "they worked together." Ruth Ann's friend, Nancy, added, "That something that really made a difference was the way they put new meaning to the word 'TOGETHER.'"

CHAPTER VII:

"DON'T SCARE THEM TO DEATH!"

A. Challenges Ahead

I asked Richard Reynolds if he had heard the rumors about Ted Smith and Ruth Ann Ward. The lights had just been turned on the baseball field at Eckerly Park for the night game for which we were getting ready. We were in the dugout after I had just warmed up Richard who was going to pitch that night. As we sat down, Bob Eadie, who plays third base, walked over and said, "Did you hear about Ted Smith and Ruth Ann Ward?"

Richard didn't answer Bob's question, and just said, "Ted is supposed to be here tonight. But he is not here yet. Don't tell us something happened to him."

"No, nothing happened to him. Ted and Ruth Ann got married a couple of weeks ago on the Saturday morning after the prom. They went to Metropolis and got married by Rev. Morris who was here at Carmi First Baptist. I didn't know if you knew about it or not."

"Got married? I thought he was going to play college football. What happened?"

Larry Kane, who was going to play second base said. "Skipworth, what the hell do you think happened? She got pregnant."

"And they got married? Where are they going to live? What are they going to do? They will be having a baby? How are they going to take care of the baby? Is Ted going to work for her dad? They are so young to have gotten married. Does this mean Ted will not go to college and play football?"

About that time, Ted pulled up in the parking lot, got out of the car, opened the door for Ruth Ann and they began to walk over to the dugout. Goob Sexton had joined us and said, "Don't ask any of those stupid ass questions, or you will scare them to death."

We all knew Ted and Ruth Ann were one of the most visible and serious couples in the high school. They could even be referred to as "The Couple." We learned that they had many conversations about what they wanted to do with their lives once they got married. The news of Ruth Ann being pregnant got around the school. Both of them responded to the gossip in a very positive way. Ruth Ann said, "Our conversations, especially after I found out I was pregnant, were about the challenges we were going to face and all the many adjustments we would have to make." The adjustments they had to make as they looked ahead were all new and foreboding. The challenge was that most everything ahead of them was going to confront a newly married teenage couple with no experience in making life changing decisions.

B. Adjustments Ahead

Adjustments? Almost everything they were facing was to be an adjustment. There was the self-avowed "spoiled rotten sixteen-year-old" who had to really adjust to almost everything that was going to happen. One would expect there to be a lot of "collateral damage" as this young couple met new challenges. In spite of having so little experience to enable them to make good decisions, they did not suffer or cause much damage.

Instead, one saw maturity in the decisions made. Especially when it came to money. Ruth Ann managed the family finances in a very responsible manner. In spite of her lack of knowledge or experience in family finances, she kept them "afloat," she kept them feeling secure and comfortable, and she made sure they were all surrounded by love.

Adjustments? Ruth Ann has spent the past seventy years fielding the question "What is for supper?" She was seldom asked to make suggestions for dinner over the course of those seventy years. She didn't have suggestions to make since she was not into cooking. In seventy years, she seldom was asked to prepare her favorite meal for the family. She was not a cook so she had no favorite meal to prepare.

Joan was asked about the meal preparations and the cooking skills of her mom. Joan said, "It is true that mom was not known for her cooking skills or interest. But we never went hungry. Mom always had meals prepared for us. Mom made sure we had enough to eat. Mom made sure that need was met."

Talk about adjustments. Working in the yard? Ask her what happened to the beautiful healthy rose bushes she planted. Adjustments don't come easy. They call for thinking, consider all the options, and making smart/astute decisions. When the instructions said, "Add one cup of fertilizer to the formula for excellent strawberries," One would think, "If one cup makes 'excellent strawberries,' two cups would make fantastic strawberries." So, why not add two cups of fertilizer? It was done. It took eight hours, and the strawberry patch which was to yield the biggest and best batch of luscious red strawberries was burned up from too much fertilizer.

C. They Made It

For a long time, experience and evidence show that most teenage marriages that take place due to pregnancy, do not make it. Even after a few months of marriage, very few couples have the "staying power" to make it work. I can't imagine what I would do if I was to have been married at seventeen. I don't even have the capacity to imagine the many facets of that role.

Ted and Ruth Ann, and other teenage married couples like them, faced so much uncertainty and anxiety. So, what was it that put Ted and Ruth Ann on a trajectory of success before all their peers? Why were they able to maneuver around all the obstacles and challenges that faced them? What did they do to make it seventy years and still be going strong?

What was said, done, or practiced that conveyed the kind of relationship they had? What took place between them that showed observers what they thought about each other? Joan described their relationship in those "moments" as she witnessed their interaction with each other. They had ways that were nondescript but personal to them, and how those special ways confirmed their love for each other. There were wordless descriptions that told their love for each other; a "pat on the rear" and their own particular nonverbal ways to say "I love you." There were always comments of an enduring nature that spoke volumes of their "covenant" to each other. In addition to the physical expressions that showed their love for each other, they never stopped saying, "I love you." Jan and Joan confirmed the common denominator, "They just put each other first."

From the very beginning, Ted and Ruth Ann considered their relationship special. As their relationship developed, they raised questions, thoughts, and issues that reflected thoughtfulness and maturity for a couple in their teens. They made statements like "What is going on with us is our business." "We will make the decisions on what we do" "We will carry on as we planned." When Ruth Ann revealed she was pregnant, they both talked about "carrying on with our plans." Ruth Ann put it all in perspective when she told everyone, "We decided to go on with what we had planned, and that is what we were going to do."

After their wedding in Metropolis, they began thinking about their move and life in Decatur at Millikin University. Ruth Ann and Jan moved to Decatur after Jan's birth in October. *Then fifteen months later, Joan was born into this young family.* Ted was one of the few college football players in the country who was putting diapers on two babies, caring for a wife, going to school, and being one of the most valuable football players in the school's history. How many college football players take a shower after practice or a game and say, "I have to hurry home. I have to warm the formula and I have diapers to change."

D. Four Married Football Players

Ted and Ruth Ann said that they knew of only three other players who were married. Those players didn't have any children, but they were of the rare number of married students on the Millikin campus. What made Ted and Ruth Ann stand out as one of the few married couples was the presence of the girls, Jan and Joan.

Ted knew changes were in store for them. For one thing, they would have to adjust to living in a new environment, being away from home, surrounded by new faces, having a different daily schedule, not having a familiar routine as in high school, and making daily decisions on their own. Add to that a wife and two babies and being only seventeen years of age and added to all that is assuming the multi-faceted of being a father. Talk about changes in store!

It is not only the changes that Ted and Ruth Ann would be experiencing, but the ripple effect this young and unique family will have on the college campus. And, what will the influence of a college campus environment be on them? Will their unique first-time exposure to Millikin University student population affect them? Will this young couple from Carmi, Illinois be able to adjust to campus life? Will it be overwhelming? Or, will it be nothing compared to the challenge they have already encountered?

CHAPTER VIII:

THE SECOND ADDITION

A. Joan Makes Her Appearance

Ruth Ann did not expect to be pregnant at age sixteen. Ted didn't expect it. Nobody expected it. Ted and Ruth Ann had no plans to be parents so soon. The first baby, Jan, was not according to their plans. Since those plans did not pan out, it was said, with great thoughtfulness, "It would be a long time before another child is born," was the oft repeated word in the Smith household. So, blame it on the position of the sun, or the brightness of the moon, or the tide in the Indian Ocean, or the Equator being bent one hundredth of a centimeter, or the earth's axis being tilted one tenth of one degree to the right, Ruth Ann got pregnant again and fifteen months later Joan joined them.

Two babies for this couple who were not even old enough to join the U. S. Army. Not old enough to get a shot of vodka at the Carmi Corner Bar. They couldn't even vote. They couldn't even buy a car from Finch Ford on Main Street in Carmi. They weren't even old enough to get a boat license to cruise up the Little Wabash to Maunie.

This very special time in the lives of Ted and Ruth Ann came at the same time a good friend of Ted's, Bob O'brien a former teammate on the football team came from St. Louis, to visit. After a variety of topics of conversation, Bob mentioned how he wanted to do something, and soon, to make some extra money. Draft was looming on the horizon facing most young men, so to make his military experience worthwhile, Bob took what would be the highest paying job in the army: a paratrooper! "Great experience," he told Ted.

As Bob was visiting this young married couple, and sharing his experiences of being a paratrooper, he told them, "Well, you have this one baby, Jan is a real blessing to you. She is so lucky to have two parents like you." Then, **he was about to say to them**, "NOW, DON'T MAKE A STUPID-ASS MISTAKE LIKE GETTING PREGNANT AGAIN. NOT FOR A WHILE, ANYWAY. THAT IS SOMETHING YOU DON'T NEED RIGHT NOW."

As Bob was about to say that word of warning, Ted interrupted him and said, "And guess what, Ruth Ann is pregnant again."

When Joan was born, the event became somewhat of a campus occasion. The "pump was primed," and had been for several months in anticipation of the second daughter of Ted and Ruth Ann. Ted was at a track meet in St. Louis. He was not there because he was being thoughtless or inconsiderate or negligent of Ruth Ann at the time of the birth of the baby. They both had gone to the doctor the day before the track meet, and Ted was very direct in his question to the doctor, "I have a track meet tomorrow and if the baby comes soon, maybe I should stay home with Ruth Ann." The doctor replied, "No, don't you worry. Go on to your track meet. The baby won't be coming for another two weeks."

The doctor said not to worry. Therefore, the next day, Ted went to the track meet. Then, in spite of what the doctor said, Ruth Ann began to have labor pains. How was Ruth Ann supposed to handle this predicament? She was home alone with one baby and one on the way. So much for the doctor's predictions! What should she do? What CAN she do? Ted had made the wise decision of putting four of his fraternity brothers on high alert just in case Ruth Ann went into labor.

She called the "captain" of the four fraternity brothers who Ted designated to be on high alert and told him, "I am experiencing some very familiar signs taking place in my body." She told him, "Get over here, and I mean in a hurry, and get me to the hospital." The four TKE fraternity brothers rushed to the apartment, three of them helped her gather her bags, helped her in the car, and took her to the hospital. One of the fraternity brothers stayed with baby Jan.

The receptionist at the hospital took Ruth Ann's name and all the intake information and finished by asking, "Which one of you three men is the father?" Ruth Ann told her, "Oh none of these men is the father. The father is out running around." The nurse thought to herself, "Oh, so sad that she is here without him, her husband must be such an uncaring person. It is a good thing that her friends are taking care of her."

Next Ruth Ann and her entourage of men folk went to the next desk which was the OBGYN department nurse. The first question Ruth Ann was asked was, "Which one of these gentlemen is the father?" By this time Ruth Ann was close to pushing the panic button. She replied to the nurse's question, "Take your pick. I don't know. And I don't care." The nurse felt sorry for her and the apparent lack of interest of the men with her and said, "Come with me." They went to Ruth Ann's room and she was handed over to the attending labor room nurse. The nurse asked her, "Where is the father?" Ruth Ann had heard enough of that question and told the nurse, "Oh I don't know, but they should be coming soon."

She got to her bed, and had to go to the toilet. The nurse was going to assist her but got a call and had to leave. As she was leaving Ruth Ann's room, the three fraternity brothers came in. The nurse said, "One of you fathers take your wife to the bathroom." One did!

The question the fraternity brothers had, which involved a lot of discussion and was very important to them, was "What about flowers in the room? We need to get flowers for Ruth Ann. What is a hospital room without flowers?" So, they scoured that floor of the hospital and when the coast was clear, they would mosey into a room that had lots of flowers and quietly take what they wanted and slipped back to Ruth Ann's room and presented her with beautiful arrangements of flowers. As this process continued, it seemed as if Ruth Ann had more flowers in her room than anyone in the history of Decatur General Hospital. People, as they walked past her room and looked in, you could hear them mutter, "Who is in that room? The mayor? The President of the Millikin? Look at all those lovely flowers!"

Another question that the TKE men asked, was "Shall we go get Ted?" He is in St. Louis for a track meet and if we can get in touch with him, he will want to come here to be with Ruth Ann and his baby. One of the fraternity brothers suggested they call the stadium where the track meet was being held and have them page Ted that a car from Decatur was coming to pick him up.

With that suggestion, one of the TKE brothers volunteered to rush to St. Louis to get Ted. And it was done. Ted was notified of the news and met his fraternity brother outside the stadium and they RUSHED to the hospital in Decatur. The fraternity brother who picked up Ted said, "It was the fastest I have ever driven a car. At one point we were about to pass a car and as we began to pass the car, a car pulled into the lane we were in to pass. We had to go off into the shoulder and then got back on the highway. Talk about scared. But we made it, and Ted got to see the baby right after she was delivered."

To make the evening momentous which was centered on an event said to be the most wonderful miracle ever to be, Ruth Ann's mother left Carmi with a boatload of food and baby toys and clothes, not knowing Ruth Ann was in the hospital awaiting her second baby. Her mother left on a bus from Carmi, when she arrived in Decatur she took a cab from the bus station to the Smith's apartment, and found a fraternity-brother babysitter watching Jan while Ruth Ann was in the hospital.

Ruth Ann's mom took another cab to the hospital and got to the hospital about the time Ted arrived, to the complete but wonderful surprise to Ruth Ann. It was a grand display of family joy to have everyone there; mom, husband, grandmother, baby, "pseudo-fraternity dads," and assorted nurses.

B. New Dimensions of Campus Activity

No, nothing will be the same anymore at the Smith apartment. Nothing will be the same on the campus of Millikin University. From now on the references will be around and toward "Teddy Smith's girls." When someone makes a comment about the Smith Army-Quonset-hut-apartment on the campus of Millikin University, they would not be referring to Ted Smith, outstanding football player, or Ruth Ann, his young beautiful wife, but they would be referring to the home of Teddy Smith's girls.

The news and the attraction of Teddy Smith's girls found its way through most of the campus. The notoriety of the girls was ever present. Jan and Joan were the subject of conversation which took place more than once. What better time to be reminded of the role of Ted Smith on the campus of Millikin University than on a Saturday afternoon home football game? More specifically, the concession stands at a home Millikin football game.

The incident goes down in the classic memorable moments of the Millikin archives of historical enclaves. Right above the main concession stand of Millikin's football stadium, is the grand-stand seating. From this vantage point, Mom, in this case, the mother of Jan and Joan, could see the wide-ranging view of the concession stand. The first time Jan and Joan ventured down to the concession stand, Ruth Ann watched with a keen eye. All the way down the stadium stairs, Jan stretched her neck to look into the concession stand, and after coming away with their treats, they rejoined their mother.

After a trip to the concession stand, Jan came back to her mom with wide-eyed wonderment, "Mom, guess what, that man who sells the popcorn, asked me. 'Are you and your sister Teddy Smith's girls? Mom, are we Teddy Smith's girls? I told him we were and he said, "There is no charge for Teddy Smith's girls."

How many college football players have a captive audience made up of his own children and extended family at one of his games? Very few, if any. How many college football players have their own toddler children running onto the field calling for "daddy, daddy?" Very few, if any. How many college football players have to leave their study of Sociology 101for a few minutes to warm up the baby formula. Only one, I ever heard of.

It is not very often that a Millikin University student athlete had his participation in a game disrupted by the sudden appearance of a baby girl making it onto the football field to find her daddy. Not many times has any college or university athlete had his or her baby trot onto the field or court calling for "Daddy, Daddy." Jan Smith, Ted's oldest daughter (about two years old at the time) meandered from her place in the West Main Stand of the football stadium, unbeknownst by her mother, and waddled onto the field trying to find her dad. She kept calling out "Daddy, Daddy." Two players saw her coming toward them and they yelled at Ted, "Ted, is that baby girl coming onto the field your Jan?"

With that question yelled at the top of the teammate's lungs, Ted ran over to Jan, picked her up and carried her over to the West Main Stand to place her in her mom's arms, all the time receiving kisses, hugs, and smiles from his main admirer, baby Jan. When he arrived at the bleacher area, the crowd erupted in a standing crescendo of cheers, not only for the star halfback for Millikin, but also for the "Daddy-of-the-Year!"

One evidence of the wide range of popularity of Jan and Joan Smith was the way they both had a first-name relationship with some of the campus staff persons: custodians, faculty, and other university personnel. The unique role they had on campus enabled Jan and Joan to become acquainted with the residents of sororities and fraternities.

The Mail Room also became a place where the girls felt welcomed and important. Walt Witt was in charge of the mail room and he soon became, not only acquainted, but enamored with the Smith girls. Walt began to keep prize candies handy in his cabinet drawer for the girls when they came to the mail room. When the girls came into Walt's work area, they headed for the bottom drawer of his cabinet. A special routine which became very familiar and expected, was the invitation from Walt to the girls to check out the bottom drawer of the cabinet.

The Tau Kappa Epsilon fraternity invited the Smith family over for a Christmas event. The fraternity had arranged for a Santa Claus to appear at a gathering of several invited students. Especially invited for the occasion were Jan and Joan. The fraternity had arranged to have Santa come into the house through the front window. When Jan and Joan saw Santa coming through the window they got scared and became very upset. They began to cry and everyone took notice. With that unexpected turn of events, Santa did a quick turn around and climbed back through the window and left. That took care of the Christmas celebration at the TKE House.

That frightening experience with Santa at the TKE House did not end the visits from Jan and Joan. It was no surprise that the cook at the Tau Kappa Epsilon fraternity house, "Grandma," began to cater to the girls the more they made their presence felt at the TKE House. Often, when Jan and Joan would visit the fraternity with their dad, Grandma would have the girls in the kitchen and would make available to them, pots and pans and wooden spoons to bang on the pots and pans. It became expected that everywhere the girls went, they were never left aside or neglected in any way.

A special fun experience that the Smith girls had that relates to their TKE contact, were the times the girls would head up to the dorm at the fraternity to rustle up the brothers from their beds. "It is time to get up and get to school." The commotion that came from the attic dorm was from the exciting surprise, the welcoming encounter, and the fun amazement when these two- and three-year-old girls assumed "wake up" duties at the TKE House as their responsibility. After realizing what was going on, it was heard said by one brother, "It's those Smith girls again, and they still didn't bring any breakfast."

Pi Phi sorority was across the street from the Smith's apartment. On the way to and from classes, the sorority girls would see Jan and Joan outside in front of the apartment playing. Jan and Joan became the attraction as the students passed by. It didn't take long for the Smith girls to become the "young friends," and invited guests, and welcomed visitors to the sororities.

The main benefit with all the attention to Jan and Joan? Babysitting. Ted and Ruth Ann did not have much time, money, or opportunity to "go out," but with all the volunteers who wanted to be babysitters, they found some time. One sorority girl became a special invited guest to the Smith apartment. She was a Japanese student by the name of Masaka Toyota. She became very close to the girls and was their most frequent babysitter. As the relationship grew, Masaka gave the Smith's a handmade Christmas gift, a porcelain bell ornament for the Christmas tree. Ted says, "It is a very special handcrafted ornament, and we have placed it on top of the Christmas tree for almost seventy years. It has become a special family favorite."

Not only did the sororities and fraternities come to know the Smith girls, but the faculty meetings also had a contact with them. Faculty luncheon meetings were held not far from the Smith apartment and often, leftover food was taken down to the Smith apartment from the faculty meetings.

One never knew where the next "hand-out" would come from. Every visitor seemed to know that if you went to the Smith's, you better be prepared to bring an offering to the girls. Adam Russell, 6'2" and 300 lb lineman learned the hard way that you better pay attention to the girls. In a rather nonchalant way of coming over to visit between classes, he came in holding a quart of strawberry ice cream and a spoon. He greeted the girls and they looked very expectant at the quart of strawberry ice cream. He sat down and began to dig into the ice cream. The girls stood in front of him and began to watch. He dug into the ice cream and ate. The girls continued to wait expectantly. He finished the quart of ice cream and sat comfortably for a moment.

The girls, in spite of their faces saying, "What about us?", never got offered a spoonful of ice cream. As Ruth Ann was watching this scene unfold, finally told him, "Adam, the next time you come over here with a quart of ice cream, make sure you bring enough for the girls. Don't ever come over here and eat a quart of ice cream in front of the girls again." The girls just looked at him as if to say, "Yea, and don't you forget what our mom said."

It was if a light bulb went off in his head, and he said, "Oh my gosh, I am so sorry. Jan and Joan, what is your favorite flavor of ice cream?" Ruth Ann spoke up and said, "Strawberry, what do you think?" He got up from his seat and said, "You girls go in the kitchen and get a couple of spoons. I will be right back!"

The same sharing of food was made on occasion from the football training table to the Smith home as the relationships became more popular and appreciated. The training table was available for about two weeks prior to the start of school and the football schedule. Some days, when one of the football players could not take in the meal at the training table, he would give his meal ticket to Ted so he could bring the girls and Ruth Ann. It was not only a treat for the girls to eat at the training table, but it was a treat for many of the players to join them and eat with them.

Yes, a boatload of instances of *"things are different now"* took place on campus because of the interesting presence of the Smith household. It was a unique tradeoff the college students experienced with the inclusion of the Smith girls.

This extraordinary experience of the Smith girls and the dynamic they brought to that small college campus was mainly through the steadfast presence of their mother. Ruth Ann brought a fresh and vibrant personality to fashion relationships that attracted the students, most of them older than her, but popular to them all. Ruth Ann made the impression that "she was always there." In spite of her age, inexperience, and role of housewife, mother, and not a student, Ruth Ann was a strong and dependable *'constant.'*

CHAPTER IX:

RUTH ANN TAKES OVER

A. Academic/Family Responsibilities

As with most married college students, the expectations are that the spouse, who is not the student, would assist in the class academic exercises and preparations of assignments on the scholastic side. The spouse could type term papers, help with exam preparation, proofread papers, give mock quizzes for exams, and assist in the many tasks to help the student in the family. But the circumstances were different for this married college student couple. It would be safe to guess that no married couple (with children) in the history of Millikin University were as young as Ted and Ruth Ann Smith.

First, not only were they young, but they added to their challenge with another baby in fifteen months of the first. So, Ruth Ann, instead of typing term papers, spent her time washing and folding diapers. Instead of prepping her husband with questions as he was preparing for an exam, she gave him answers when he asked questions about the baby's schedule for eating. Instead of proofreading his essay for business law, she was reading the labels on the baby formula.

One must remember, by the time Ruth Ann had matured into a woman, mother, wife, and housekeeper, she was only seventeen. Ted was only eighteen. Dividing up family tasks and responsibilities around the house were not something with which a very young married couple had any experience. The more demanding responsibility and by far the most important task, was being a parent. Being a parent was certainly something for which they also had no experience. In fact, being a parent is something for which no training is required or expected. There was no prospective parenting class to attend. Being a parent is something for which a license is not required. Talk about a challenge! Talk about "What do I do now?" Quite an adjustment for a "spoiled rotten sixteen-year-old girl" and her seventeen-year-old husband.

Therein lies the mystery! What took this naïve, inexperienced, and spoiled rotten sixteen-year-old into conduct that reflected the savvy of a mature adult? How did she shed that cloak of being a "confused lost high school junior class girl" to be making responsible decisions about feeding two babies on a particular schedule. It is as if something inside her kicked in and said, "Wake up! This is serious business now. Don't mess this up."

The mystery was manifest in the response of the athletic community at Millikin to the unique presence of the Smith girls. Where on any college campus will one find the charm, fascination, and magic that "Teddy's girls" gave to the Millikin campus? Where, in the world, will one find such a unique story to enhance the spirit of a college campus? Ruth Ann made it happen.

It is not necessary to list all the responsibilities to which a parent of a few months old baby must pay attention. But two babies? No, the last thing Ruth Ann needed was to review and proofread Ted's English Literature paper on *"The Pros and Cons of Raising Teenage Daughters."* The last thing Ruth Ann needed was to listen and critique and hear him practice his speech for Creative Speech 101, on *"I Should Have Been A Monk."*

B. Ruth Ann as Housekeeper

One time Ruth Ann took charge of painting one of the walls in their apartment. She did a fine job. The paint application was done with quality workmanship. The problem was she had mixed the "water based" paint with the "oil based" and it seemed to smear in streaks without covering the wall consistently. Ted told her, the color selection was beautiful.

But Ruth Ann had a "touch" for painting. She had a way of fashioning a style, a way, a pattern that expressed creativity. As she and Jan eventually made their way to Decatur, Ruth Ann brought with them a small contribution of Ruth Ann for the apartment. Ruth Ann took orange crates, painted them a bright yellow, and placed them in their apartment. What else would a teenage couple do with a new baby when the purse strings are limited. The crates served a grand purpose – living room décor.

Cooking was not her most favorite household chore. Cooking was also not her most favorite interest. But she tried to venture into preparation of a meal that her family would enjoy and give her accolades for the accomplishment of the finished product. She made some homemade soup. She served the hot soup in a fashion fit for a gourmet cook. The only problem was she served the hot soup in wooden lacquered bowls. Of course, the bowl of hot soup turned into a lacquered tasting soup. Not everyone was required to "clean your plate." Those who did, found the soup slid down with ease.

Raising two girls in 1953-1954 was not during the time of "conveniences," "time saving devices," "accommodating tools," "amenable," or "ease" or "comfort." In other words, *disposable diapers* were not included as a part of the routine of life for this mother of two. So, when she saw an ad for "Two months free trial of disposable diapers with the purchase of life insurance," she jumped on that offer! No matter what she had to do to earn that two-month trial, she was on it. They had plenty of life insurance and plenty of diapers.

Her friends said they were amazed at the many tasks she undertook when she did so few domestic chores growing up. Remember how she told them that she was a "spoiled kid?" Well, her inexperience showed. Her friends were privy to the time she put Ted's jeans on a rack to stretch them after washing them. Then she put starch on them to make them look nice. But she could hardly get them off the rack!

She planted tomato plants and was proud of the design and order of a picturesque tomato patch. The quality and quantity were truly picturesque. To make it even more a model for folks to see and appreciate, she cut off the dangling "flowers." She didn't know those were the tomatoes themselves.

With Ruth Ann's interest and expertise in sewing, she suggested to the girls that they come up with an elaborate creative birthday gift idea for their dad. She told them, "With your help we will get him a dozen pair of boxer brief underwear. They will not be just a pair of underwear to replace present underwear. These finished products are to be colorful, lively, unique, and attractive to the eye."

Jan and Joan, not fully understanding what project their mom was leaning to, added to Ruth Ann's idea the thought of sewing extremely colorful cloth on each pair of boxer shorts. They wanted to purchase red and yellow ribbons, bright purple head bands, colorful cloth reflectors. Ruth Ann told the girls that after a few more "fun encounters like these with all the colors and brightness, we won't need to display the July 4 fireworks."

The girls went with their mom to pick out, not only the shorts, but the decorative material that they were to sew on each pair of shorts. Once the sewing is ready, the next task is to make sure the bright colors of material are sewed to each pair of boxer shorts.

The girls and their mom had a big laugh when they imagined Ted taking a shower after practice and putting on his "new boxer shorts" in front of all the football players with all the bright colored streamers and appointments.

Another creative idea the girls came up with was building a "snow-woman." They said all they would need to make it complete, were red life savers which could go on the "snow-woman" for her nipples.

Ruth Ann was very good at decorating. Jan says "She had a natural interest and inclination for decorating and working in the yard. I sometimes would join her working in the yard on a hot summer day. I would give up and go into the cool house and she would still be outside in the hot sun doing what she likes to do. We are alike in several ways but the biggest difference is that I am more independent than she is. I have spent a lot of time with my husband gone. I know that Mom and Dad have spent little time apart from each other. So, I think I get the nod for being more independent."

Jan says it is a treat to hear her mom when she starts reminiscing. She can remember everything and that enables you to enter her thoughts and those descriptive scenes. She helps you re-experience that moment. She puts pictures to her reminiscing as she goes into details. She makes it mesmerizing.

But what the teenage Ruth Ann lacked in knowledge and experience in being a housewife, she more than made up in her task of taking on the role of mother. As a young mother, she handled that responsibility with maturity, compassion, and a touch of wisdom that most mothers seek to possess.

How and why did she turn a huge challenge into order and stability and assurance? What made it happen? What was that inner power, that inner spirit of strength, that inner source of knowing what decisions to make and what direction to go? Ruth Ann assumed the responsibility to make it happen. The skeptics voiced their doubt.

The naysayers questioned the ability to overcome the "strikes against them." "How long will it last?" was the common question by her friends.

That which defined her role as mother in these circumstances, was her *TENACITY.* She heard the skeptics. She knew the volume of doubts that were thrown her way. She heard the questions raised about success in this new venture. But her response was to hold fast to the resolve to succeed. Joan, the daughter who described this inner motivation as *TENACITY*, said that a grand resolve was evident in Ruth Ann's confident response, "I am going to succeed!" This same resolve, this same tenacity was evident in the success that Ruth Ann made of their later venture of owning the restaurant, Two Tony's. Ruth Ann knew what to do and she did it.

From the trials of being a young mother, to the woman she was in this adventure with Ted, how do those close to her describe her? Many referred to her as "good." Not "good" in its simple term, but "good" covering many facets of the measure of a person; a friend, mother, wife, daughter, student, and support of a person who is ever present. Good, when used to describe Ruth Ann, means everything right, in place, thought through, prepared, and expecting the best. Good, as in the aspiration of others to be like her.

Probably the finest compliment and description of Ruth Ann came from so many who have known her growing up and into adulthood. "It was always fun being around Ruth Ann. She was always talking but in a way that made you feel she was talking only to you. She seemed to always be smiling. That always made us feel good, that things were OK. She seemed to always be positive and optimistic and that made us all feel good. The old cliché "When she enters the room, everything lights up." That fit Ruth Ann.

C. Ted Changes His Major

From a major in Physical Education curriculum to a major in Business, is quite a stretch. It is almost as bad a going from Physical Education to Theology! When Ted made the surprising stretch from P.E. to business, one wonders what other surprises will we find out about Ted Smith? As one finds huge changes in study choices, one could ask, what else can we find out about Ted Smith?

Everyone assumed Ted would not only play football at Millikin, but as is often the case, become a physical education major. After all, at Carmi he was an all-around athlete. So, with all those expectations laid on him, he signed up to be a physical education major. That would enable him to fulfill his participation in sports. In spite of all those expectations, coaching was something he had on his mind anyhow, for the past three years.

He enrolled in Business Administration and Management his sophomore year. Ted became acquainted with the dean of the business school, Dean Smith. He enabled Ted to no longer be under the guise of a "dumb jock." He emphasized to Ted, that he did not fit that image, but "You have smarts." Ted became to appreciate Dean Smith and all he did for him in the transition from one major to another.

In thinking about his experience at Millikin, and considering the effect of those experiences, Ted said, "I had many roles at Millikin; I was a husband, son, father of two baby girls, I was a student giving attention to studies, I was a football player, I was on the track team, I tried to take on the role to help fashion a household and family, and to be a leader to my teammates. I worked to have an on-field and off-field comradery with my teammates.

D. The Blue Mill

Their apartment on campus was located in such a place that they were exposed to a lot of student traffic. They also had a lot of attention and gazes as the students became more and more acquainted with the presence and uniqueness of two beautiful little girls. As the students passed by, they would make an occasional greeting, stop and converse for a moment, or just give a big wave and smile as they walked by.

Ruth Ann told about an incident that she took care of early on in their living on campus. "Near our apartment was a bar and hangout which was very popular with the students. It was called the Blue Mill Bar. It was just down the street from us. The sidewalk that went to its main entrance went right by our front porch. I was sitting in the swing on the front porch having a cup of coffee and this guy walked by. He was going to the Blue Mill. He looked over in my direction and saw me in the swing. He said to me, 'You are too pretty to be sitting there by yourself. A pretty girl like you ought to go with me to the Blue Mill and have a drink.'

I had my coffee cup in my hand and I threw it at him. I missed and the cup smashed into a carton of Coke bottles sitting on the top rail of the porch. They all fell off the railing and they shattered all over. He stopped and had a look of shock and amazement. He couldn't believe what he just saw. I yelled at him, 'Get your ass out of here and don't ever come by this house again.' The guy took off in a run to the Blue Mill. I never saw him come by the house again."

CHAPTER X:

DETOUR TO HOUSTON

A. Why Houston?

R uth Ann said that at the end of Ted's junior at Millikin the family had just about enough of spartan living. "We were hungry a lot of the time, in fact, we were hungry most of the time. We didn't go out much or do much because it would cost us and we couldn't afford it. We spent a lot of time at home just taking care of things at home, things we could do.

"We had plenty of offers for babysitters from fraternity brothers, sorority girls, football players, coeds, and other students. But we never had to money to go out. We had plenty of company with all the students that came by. We hardly ever had a day go by that we didn't have a visitor at our apartment, we never felt lonely. In spite of that, and in spite of the many offers to have babysitters, our social outings for entertainment were very limited.

"Ted's brother lived in Houston and had a good job. When he heard us complain about not having any money, he invited us down to Houston to look around, see how we liked it, and find a good paying job. After thinking about it for a few weeks, at the end of the first semester of Ted's junior year, we decided to take the risk, the chance."

The "risk," the "chance," became a confident and determined decision for the Smiths. How sure were they? While living in Decatur, they grew attached to a piece of furniture that became a treasured item for the family. It was a full-length mirror that the girls took full advantage in front of which they did their "modeling." The mirror was even used for their artistic efforts.

So, the mirror became a part of the load on the trailer on the long haul to Houston. As the road got longer and the load began to settle, one piece of the load began to rattle and shake and make a very annoying noise. After a couple of tries to rearrange and stop the noise, the annoyance continued as they got back on the road.

As the racket continued the further they drove, the more annoyed Ted became. They stopped at a bridge over a river, Ted got out of the car, went back to the load of furniture, picked out the problem piece of furniture and threw it over the bridge railing into the river. Ruth Ann asked, "What was the offending piece of furniture you threw into the river?" Ted told her and the girls, "That damn mirror." Ruth Ann yelled at him, "When we get to Texas, I am going to get one of those six foot three, two-hundred-pound Texas lawyers and divorce your sorry *&^^%."

When Ted pulled the car onto the highway, Ruth Ann leaned over to him and kissed him and said, "You know, I love you so much that I will just take the girls out and we will find ourselves another mirror."

B .Living In Houston

Ted told the story of their time in Houston, "We spent three years in Houston. I found a good job at TBC Chemical Company for a while and was given the chance to work overtime. I usually made more in overtime money than I did in my regular hours. The chemical company job didn't last long since I didn't know anything about chemicals. I had the job of being with a team of workers digging a ditch to put in a special line at the plant. It took several of us men digging the line because they didn't have room to get a tractor in the area. The next place I found work was a company called Mueller's. It was at Mueller's that I was able to work more hours, make more money, and just did manual labor.

"Let me tell you about a real adventure in our time spent in Houston. I was driving around, on the campus of the University of Houston and I noticed what looked like the track team practicing. I stopped to watch. It turned out to be the University of Houston track team. The place I parked my car happened to be near the high jump pit so I watched the high jumpers.

"When I got closer, I noticed a man who appeared to be the coach. I heard him give pointers to a couple of the jumpers. I asked him if I could demonstrate to one of the jumpers the technique he was trying to explain. He said, 'Sure, have at it.' He didn't notice the work boots I had on. He also didn't seem to notice I had on my Khaki work pants and a tee shirt.

"I talked to the jumper he had addressed earlier and demonstrated the technique the coach was trying to explain. I made the jump which was at a height the varsity jumpers had trouble maneuvering. 'Do you mind if I do a couple more jumps with your jumpers?' By this time, he saw my work boots and he replied to my question, 'You can jump all day, if you want.' He must have thought I was some jerk who came off the street who needed to be told to keep my mouth shut.

"I took off my work boots and socks and took a couple of more jumps. I asked the coach to raise the bar. It was now at the height the varsity jumpers were using. I jumped that height and even higher. The high jumping style I used then was not the Fosbury Flop. The Fosbury Flop became famous and the most popular technique later. I used the standard Western Roll. After two more successful jumps, the coach forgot about the hayseed with work boots.

"The coach asked me where I was from. I told him Illinois. He asked me if I was in a hurry. I told him no. He asked me if I had any experience in sports, especially track and field. I told him yes. He asked if I had ever competed in sports, especially track and field. I told him yes. He asked if I had ever competed in college. I told him I had attended Millikin University in Illinois and competed in track and field. But I had left after my junior year to come to Houston to work. He asked me to go with him to see the Athletic Director.

"We entered a building with a long hallway and offices on either side. As we walked down the hallway, a voice called out from one of the offices, 'Ted Smith, is that you?' I couldn't believe it, someone way down here in Houston, Texas knew my name. It turned out to be a former professor from Millikin who was now teaching at the University of Houston. He asked me what I was doing down there. I told him I came down to work. The track coach recognized him and told him we were going to the AD's office to inquire about a track scholarship. The coach asked him if he wanted to join us. He said, 'Absolutely.'

"When we walked into the AD's office, the coach told him about our meeting at the high jump pit and that I out-jumped the team's high jumpers. He told the AD 'We should offer him a scholarship.' The former Millikin professor who accompanied us to the AD's office, spoke up and said, 'And if you don't offer him a scholarship for track, I can tell you that if you offer him a scholarship for football, you will never have a better running back than Ted Smith. I know, because I was teaching at Millikin University in Decatur, Illinois and Ted Smith carried the team.'"

C. "Finish Your Degree"

"After more conversation about attending the University of Houston, and the opportunity for scholarship help, the AD suggested we check on my academic standing at Millikin and the possibility of getting the transfer of my transcript. In just a short time the transcript came. It showed I would have to take six courses in order for me to become eligible to compete in sports at the University of Houston. I did not want to spend another span of time to become eligible with an extra load of courses to take. I told them thanks, but that I would just return to Millikin and complete my degree there."

D. Family's Feelings About Houston

Jan and Joan left a very vivid and demonstrative theological imprint of their time in Houston and specifically, their time at First Baptist Church of Houston. In the decades of the 50's and 60's, smoking was permitted inside most buildings and public places. Jan and Joan took that initiative and pressed it against the policies and procedures of First Baptist Church.

Each Sunday was their day to rest, relax, come down off the busy demanding task of being preschoolers. So, on Sunday mornings during worship service, they would sit in the pew and lay back, relax, and have a smoke. They smoked their own brand of cigarettes. They tore the worship folder into small strips of paper with which they made their cigarettes. They coordinated and timed their smoking with the liturgy so they would know when to lite-up. They wanted the offering plates passed down their pew onto which they would flick their ashes. They never made a sound, they never seemed to flout it with others in the pew, they didn't blow smoke in the face of others, they just had their smokes and never bothered anybody. Although Jan and Joan left this ecclesiastical practice for other preschoolers to carry on, no one has yet to take up the mantle of following the footsteps of Teddy's girls at First Baptist Church of Houston.

How did the family feel about leaving Houston? Tears that were shed provided the "lubricant" to the readiness to leave. The tears came about by a very touching and loving letter sent from Ruth Ann's mother. Only a grandmother's letter could elicit such a feeling of sadness and guilt and need to comfort a grandmother of two beautiful and loved granddaughters as the words sent by Ruth Ann's mom.

Ruth Ann's response? "Let's get back to Millikin." Ted asked, "Do you want to go back and have me finish up and graduate? I have one more year of eligibility left and just a few hours to be able to graduate." Ruth Ann replied, "We have nothing here to hold us. And I know what my mother would want us to do."

CHAPTER XI:

LAST YEAR AT MILLIKIN

A. The Millikin Standout

His senior year, the football team was headed for an undefeated season. They won six straight games. In their second to last game, the eventual conference champions beat Millikin handily 35 to 6. Millikin could still tie for the conference championship if they won their last game. They lost the last game against Carrol by one point. The kicker missed the extra point try.

Even though he was one of the best running backs in the conference, ranking first in the conference in scoring, and second in total yards gained, and averaging 5.2 yards per carry, he wasn't always at the top of his game. Ryan Jorstad, a teammate and defensive lineman, tells the story of Ted breaking free for a huge gain and a possible touchdown. He was out-running tacklers and seeing daylight, only to trip over his feet and miss the opportunity to really draw the crowd to its feet. It happens!

At the film session of the replays of the game, when everyone saw Ted's tripping and falling hard on the turf, the players could not hold back the laughter and choice comments. The incident was heightened with the laughter from the coach.

The football coach at Millikin when Ted arrived in 1953 was soft spoken, did not yell, and was not a big talker kind of coach. He would be referred to by some, as gentle but authoritative; he let the players have some rope to make some decisions, but he was the final decision maker; he was never loud, but people listened when he spoke; he never gave the impression he was the "boss," but he was a winning coach who was in charge. Ted says, "Coach Allen was the best thing for me and us as a couple and family."

Ted tells of the incident that took place during a practice that involved Coach Allen. At the time, the helmets had just a single bar over the face as the face guard. In more recent times, the face guard covers and protects the face completely. On a practice play Ted was tackled, and a cleat from the tackler's shoes got under Ted's face guard and put a hole in Ted's chin. Ted said the blood really started coming out all over.

After the play, Ted took off his helmet and slammed it against the bench. Coach Allen saw what Ted had done in response to being bloodied on the play and said, "Ted there is a big difference between a GOOD football player and a GREAT football player. A GREAT football player will not throw his helmet." As time went on, I paid close attention to Coach Allen's demeanor, his grace, his maturity, and the respect he had from everyone. He impressed me so much that it affected my behavior, my attitude, and how I relate to and treat other people. Everyone in my family learned from Coach Allen.

"A great football player will not throw his helmet." "Those words have rung in my head all these years. When Coach Allen said that to me, it was if a spontaneous transformation took place." Ted would compare it to a light bulb going off in his head. The demeaner, the voice of calm and assurance that came from Coach Allen really was absorbed by Ted. All of a sudden, he understood clearly what the coach had meant. Then a calm set in. Ted picked up his helmet wiped the blood off and put it back on and then walked over to the coach and said, "I want to be a great player." Nothing else needed to be said.

"My last year at Millikin was a significant year. My former high school coach, Don Shroyer had become the new head football coach at Millikin in 1958. Shroyer was a great halfback for Millikin in the last few years of the decade of the forties and the first couple of years of the 50's. He was one of seven football player from Millikin drafted by the NFL. He was drafted by the Chicago Bears, but his NFL career was cut short due to an injury."

Shroyer's new college coaching experience became special because he was reunited with one of his most valuable players from his high school coaching career, Ted Smith. The concern that came to everyone's mind was, "With Ted's former high school coach now the head football coach at Millikin, Ted Smith will have a free ride. Ted will be the premier player, now."

That feeling by some led to all kinds of rumors and insinuations of the role of Ted Smith on his return to Millikin after an absence of three years. There were some on the team that would be having conversation and when Ted would come close, they ceased the conversation. There was resentment, animosity, and even apparent dismissal of Ted by some of the players. One of the halfbacks, who was designated to be a starter, was too vigorous in his animosity toward Ted. "He has been out of activity for three years and he comes back with Shroyer here to find his old place. Who does he think he is?"

That was not the case. Ted Smith had been the premier player on the Millikin football team. The coach, whoever he might be, had nothing to do with the role Ted Smith had with this team. No one who ever played with Ted voiced such a thought. Ted Smith has proven who he is (everybody associated with Millikin football knows who Ted Smith is), what he can do (and everybody associated with Millikin football knows what Ted Smith has done), and what kind of teammate he is (everybody associated with Millikin football knows the team is always better when Ted Smith is on it).

One of the players who was in his second year on the team made a comment that brought the ire of one of the veterans on the team. He made an accusatory comment about "the player from southern Illinois who has free reign since Shroyer is the coach." In an instant, the veteran player walked up to him, leaned into his face and spoke directly, eyeball to eyeball. In a very slow deliberate manner, with clarity, quietly engaging each player to listen as he enunciated each word, spoke in a voice fit for a funeral benediction, *"Don't every say anything negative about Ted Smith around here. Millikin football is Ted Smith football. He made it that way long before any of us got here. The only way you speak about Ted Smith is with respect and appreciation."*

B. Last Season for Football for Ted Smith

"I never set any goals for myself for each of the seasons I played at Millikin. I just had the attitude that I would just do my best. Whatever I accomplished by doing my best, that would be what was done." When it was mentioned to him that he was often referred to as "Millikin's standout" and what did he think of that label? He said, "I was also called one you could depend on. I really appreciated that label. All the accolades I got came from me doing one thing; when the coach said, 'Go do it.' I did everything I could to get it done."

Ted Smith played four years of football at Millikin. He was highly recruited and when he settled on Millikin, he was not assured of a starting position. During his freshman year at Millikin, he sat on the bench the first game of his first season. He entered as a sub the second game and ran one play, although he did not carry the ball. In the second half he entered again as a sub. This time the play which was called was a running play with Ted carrying the ball. He broke for fifty-four yards for a touchdown. From that play on, Ted was the starting halfback for Millikin.

How did Ted fair as a college football player? He played both defense and offense. His best position was on offense as a halfback. He did well at Millikin as a running back and as a defensive back. As a senior he made the second team all-conference as an offensive player. In 1955, as a junior, he made the second team all-conference on both defense and offense.

Jerry Domescik played tailback as a freshman in the backfield with Ted who was a senior. Domescik says that Ted was respectfully referred to as the "old man." He quickly adds, "But he was a role model for all of us with his leadership and maturity." Domescik recalls being in the backfield with Ted playing wingback. "I loved playing with him in the backfield when he was flankered right or left. The middle linebacker would shift with him producing a wide open off tackle slant the opposite way for me to run through for big yardage or even a touchdown. He definitely played a big factor in my success as a freshman."

Several years later, long after graduation, Coach Shroyer died. There was a special recognition of him at the first football game after his death. Several of his players were invited back for the memorable occasion. With Ted and Ruth Ann's invitation, Ted asked to add two good friends and neighbors from Carmi, Lance Leithliter and his wife, Terri. Ted called the host of the reunion and gathering of former players to ask if he could bring his friends. Ted was told it was a very special and private gathering of those who were associated with Coach Shroyer and guests were not expected to attend.

About an hour later, Ted received a phone call from the host and he told Ted, "After further thought, if you want to bring your friends, by all means, do so." Ted asked him what would be the charges for his friends to take advantage of all the social functions that had a fee. The host replied, "There will be no extra charge, that will all be taken care of. We will be glad to have them."

After all the weekend festivities were completed, Ted and Ruth Ann, Lance and Terri headed home to Carmi. As they were driving home, Lance said to Ted, "Ted, you are the first celebrity I have ever had the pleasure to know."

CHAPTER XII:

MOVING BACK TO CARMI

A. Stop off at Terra Haute

After graduation from Millikin, Ted began a promising career with Marathon Oil. He successfully maneuvered his way through a series of interviews which found him in consideration for an extensive training program with Marathon. The training was to acquaint him with some of the specific operations within Marathon. He began his career with Marathon as a sales rep with Terra Haute, Indiana as his main office.

In just a short time with Marathon, his boss, Robert Blackburn called him to his office to offer some personal and professional advice. "Ted, I want to talk to you like a father would talk to his son. You are not a "corporate type." You have too much to offer. What you should be doing is be your own boss, possibly own your own company, strike out and be creative in your own business." He told Ted, "I think it is very important that I do all I can to help in that endeavor as well as Marathon. We will continue to pay your salary but you won't be spending your time here. You take this time we are offering you to find the job fashioned for you. Take whatever time you need, but find the right job for Ted Smith."

Ted was really surprised at the offer, but more excited about the prospects of finding something he would enjoy and at which he would be good. He also saw in the offer a bit of pressure. He had to find the right "fit," the right job with the right expectations that would meet his interests and skills. Business is the area in which he would be most comfortable, but to find the right job and the opportunity it might bring him, may be too big a challenge.

Ted spent two weeks looking for a job while still being paid a salary by Marathon Oil. After two weeks he went to his boss's office and expressed his sincere thanks for being so considerate of him and his family. Ted told him he could not continue taking a salary under these circumstances and was going to go back home to Carmi to see what discoveries he could find there. With little success in those two weeks, his boss understood and with sincere best wishes, sent Ted and his family on to their next adventure with his fondest hopes.

This change of plans did not fit with the "PROPHECY" as introduced on page 67 of the 1953 CTHS Year Book. Page 67 listed all the prophecies of the members of the graduating class of 1953. Ted Smith's prophecy was the thirteenth listed. His prophecy? It states the following; *Ted Smith eventually became head coach of Dogtown University. He coaches football, softer than softball, and a new devilish sport, "H" bomb throwing.* I have no idea what that all means or what the author tried to convey. But I am sure that as they all sat around at the Year Book distribution party, reading what other prophecies were written, and signing their autographs in each other's annual, they all had a big laugh over Ted's prophesy and their own.

B. Next Stop, Carmi

The next major decision after the opportunity with Marathon Oil, was the preparation to move back to Carmi. Ted and Ruth Ann raised the question to themselves, if we moved back to Carmi, what message would that give to all our friends and family in Carmi? What message would it give to Ruth Ann's close friends? What message would it give to all of Ted's friends who stayed in Carmi and never left in the first place? What about their friends who left Carmi but came back before Ted and Ruth Ann? They had the perfect reason to say, "I told you so." The rumors had it that "Ted and Ruth Ann couldn't make it away from Carmi." "Ted and Ruth Ann had to have her folks support them." "Ted and Ruth Ann didn't have the capacity to cut their ties to Carmi." They were stuck in the tired and worn-out cliché by some Carmi folk who didn't know Ted and Ruth Ann; "You can take Ted and Ruth Ann out of Carmi, but you can't take Carmi out of Ted and Ruth Ann." Ted and Ruth Ann had plans.

All the many questions and quiet curiosity would come to naught when the people knew what Ted had in mind in coming back to Carmi. What better omen for Carmi Township High School then to have its star running backs in the history of the school come back to teach and coach football! The die was cast. Ted attended a program in Evansville, Indiana to earn his teaching credentials as well as take on his main interest, coaching football at CTHS. What better symbol of coming "full circle" with one's life as Ted had envisioned for his.

"The decision to move back to Carmi was a mutual decision made between me and Ruth Ann. No decision was ever made by one of us, without a thorough and thoughtful conversation between the two of us. Every decision, major or not, was made mutually. We never argued about it and neither of us insisted on having our own way. Our decisions were always mutual and with respect in what we said and how we said it. But, the decision to move back to Carmi, was not only going back home, but it had about it, the opportunity to take part in the second love of my life, football. My first love was and is always, my Ruth Ann.

So, we moved to Carmi and as I made preparations to teach and coach at CTHS, I also set up an insurance office in downtown Carmi. I was with Northwest Mutual Insurance from Evansville, Indiana. I was sent to be trained at a training program in Milwaukee, Wisconsin. After being certified, I opened the office."

C. Next Stop, Two Tony's

Ted sold insurance for about three months. About four or five months prior to that, two men, both named Tony, opened a buffet restaurant called "Two Tony's" on the northside of Carmi, across the Little Wabash River bridge but still in the city limits. Two Tony's had two other restaurants, one in Rolla, Missouri and another not far from Carmi, in West Frankfort, Illinois.

Ted figured he would go to Two Tony's and see if the owners would like to buy commercial insurance. As the three men were having some preliminary conversation on the subject of insurance, one of the men changed the subject and asked Ted if he would consider becoming the manager of Two Tony's. Ted told them no, that is not something he would be interested in.

Suddenly, as though a lightbulb went off in his head, he remembered the comments his boss at Marathon told him, "Ted, you have the capacity to own your own business. You need to be your own boss. You need to be in charge." Ted then did the unexpected, just out of the blue, he raised the question to the two Tonys, "Would you be interested in selling Two Tony's?"

It came as an unexpected surprise to both men to hear Ted's question. They looked at each other and said, "We have never thought of it. We don't know. We have never had that question asked of us about selling the restaurant. We don't know if we would be interested or not. Are you really serious?"

"Yes, I am very serious."

"Your question wasn't expected and caught us off guard. That is something we will have to think about. Since you are serious about it, we will have to do some thinking and let you know in a few days." With that as the closing comment in their conversation, Ted left to go talk to Ruth Ann about his offer to buy Two Tony's. There was no conversation or talk about insurance with the two Tonys.

The first reaction from Ruth Ann was shock! "Ted, I don't know holy *&%$# about cooking. And, you don't know anything about owning a business, especially a restaurant. And, where is the money going to come from to buy this place? I thought you were going to become the football coach at Carmi? What happened to that idea?"

Ted had no answer to Ruth Ann's questions. Especially the question on "Where is the money going to come from to buy Two Tony's?" About a week later, one of the two Tony's called Ted and told him they would like to talk to him about selling Two Tony's. Ted and Ruth Ann began to not only be enthused about the prospects of owning a restaurant, but began to have a vision of what they could do with Two Tony's. As they became more excited, thoughts and "off the cuff" plans seemed to roll right off their tongues and the idea of coaching at Carmi Township High School took a long second place position on "places of interest."

Instead, they talked about the buffet offerings, their roles as proprietors, working with the young people and other employees, their individual responsibilities where they could exhibit their skills and interests, uniforms, changes they were excited to make, and the general overall feeling of contributing something good and positive to their community.

Two Tony's Buffet Restaurant

D. Two Tony's in the Hands of Ted and Ruth Ann

Ted said, "We could really make it work. Together, with a lot of work and good people around us, we could have a very successful business. As far as money to make the purchase, I will go to the bank tomorrow to see what we can arrange."

Ruth Ann continued with excited expectation, "OK, we could make it THE place in Carmi and even southern Illinois! Maybe dad could help us get the financing to buy the place depending on what you find out at the bank. Remember what Blackburn told you? He said you need to own your own business. You need to be in charge. This sounds like something just made for us."

The next day Ted went to one of the local banks in Carmi. After a short conversation he found that the expectations of the bank official were going to be too hard to meet. It was a major disappointment to Ted not to get the cooperation from their own local bank, especially to one of Carmi's favorite young couples who was going to start up a business in their home town. Without skipping a beat, Ted immediately drove down to Norris City, just a few miles south of Carmi. It was in a Norris City bank that Ted found his way to make the purchase of Two Tony's. Ted talked about the cooperative way the bank dealt with him. In just that brief visit, Ted had arranged for the loan which enabled him to make the purchase of Two Tony's.

Two days later, Ted and Ruth Ann were the owners of Two Tony's restaurant. They knew nothing about the restaurant business. Ted lived in the kitchen for five months to learn all he could about cooking, preparing meals for a restaurant, the maintenance and care, and the overall expectations of managing a restaurant. The longer he lived in the kitchen, the more the kitchen employees became uncomfortable and suspicious of why he was there. Was he here to check on our work? Was he here to evaluate our commitment to working in this restaurant? He is the new owner, is he trying to find out what kind of employees we are? Is he looking us over to see if he wants to keep us on as employees?

The question came up, "What shall we name our new restaurant? We could call it 'Ted and Ruth Ann's.'" Or better yet, we could call it "J and J" or "Two Jays" after the girls." Several of their good intentioned friends offered suggestions, like in memory of good old Carmi High, "The Bulldog Pit." Or after Ted's college, "The Big Blue." Some loyalists suggested to Ted that it be called, "The Carmian." Ted and Ruth Ann listened patiently to all the suggestions and decided to keep the name Two Tony's. That name had placed the restaurant on the map. It started to have a following. "We will make Two Tony's even bigger and better and more popular than ever."

Ted felt that the time living in the kitchen would help him get acquainted with the total operation of running the restaurant. He and Ruth Ann wanted Two Tony's to be a first-class operation. He needed to find out how to use all the equipment and utensils,   what was needed, what were the tasks, responsibilities, and expectations of everybody in order to make everything work efficiently.

A big advantage that Ted and Ruth Ann had over the previous owners, was that they knew most of the people in Carmi, they had a knowledge of who had what skills that might be needed at Two Tony's, and they knew what kind of workers they would be.

Not too long after Ted spent his "indoctrination" while living in the kitchen, the original Two Tony's kitchen crew quit. So, Ted took advantage of knowing some of the local people and who could fill the needs in the kitchen.

Mae Hall came on board and worked for twenty-eight years. She was one of the backbones of the new enterprise which was still called Two Tony's. Another truly dedicated worker was Grace Coale. She too made the kitchen the source of quality that made Two Tony's the name and place to be to eat and have, not only a great meal, but an environment of comfort and the feeling of "It is good to have been here."

Another local personality that had strong roots in Carmi was Louie Mitchell's mother, Hazel. Louie Mitchell was in the CTHS class of 1955 and also a halfback, and teammate of Ted's for two years in high school and also as another teammate at halfback at Millikin. Those three ladies gave Ted and Ruth Ann's Two Tony's the local flavor and identity of a special White County enterprise. Ted and Ruth Ann began to make Two Tony's the new phenomenon of White County. Two Tony's became a local venture all the way. Two Tony's became not only the place to eat in Carmi, but the place to eat in a three-state area.

Two Tony's had become a landmark, one of the most well-known features of White County. Ted and Ruth Ann put Two Tony's on the map. Observing the license plates in the parking lot, was a real confirmation of the popularity of Two Tony's. There were several cars from all over. To get an idea of the vast scope of Two Tony's popularity, Ted and Ruth Ann were on their way to a wedding in Rolla Missouri. Just after going through St. Louis, they decided to stop at a Dairy Queen to get a bite to eat. After they placed their order, the manager of the DQ stared at Ruth Ann and said, "Are you from a restaurant called Two Tony's in Carmi, Illinois? Aren't you the hostess at the big buffet?" She said, with a great deal of surprise in her voice, "Yes, who are you?" "I had dinner with you about two weeks ago."

Often, a car load of gentlemen would pull into the parking lot of Two Tony's. They had flown into the airport in Evansville and rented a car to come to Two Tony's. Sometimes, a plane would land at the tiny airport in Carmi and passengers would get a ride to Two Tony's in the "courtesy car" the Carmi airport provided. People came from all over to taste the "homecooked" delicacies that Ted and Ruth Ann knew were going to be special selections to so many people.

One of the main or well known "homemade delicacies" was the dumplings. Ted described the process of making the dumplings in a way that would suggest they were top secret. But that is the feeling one has after getting up from the table after a great meal that includes the dumplings, "I wonder where they got the recipe for those dumplings? It was wonderful. I bet they keep that recipe under wraps."

The same can be said about the dinner rolls that really enhanced Two Tony's reputation. The hot rolls came out in big trays straight from the oven. People would wait in line for another tray of rolls to come out after a tray became empty.

Who came the furthest to eat at Two Tony's? One car load of gentlemen came all the way from New Mexico. They were on their way by car to an event on the East coast. As they were preparing for their trip east, the person helping them prepare their route, noticed they would be going on route 460 through Illinois. "When you get on route 460 through Illinois, you have to stop at the best buffet restaurant in several states. It is in Carmi, Illinois and is called Two Tony's. That is a must for you."

Ted and Ruth Ann had made Two Tony's the place to visit and have a great meal when visiting or driving through southern Illinois. It became one of the most famous buffets in that part of the state. People would drive for miles to eat at Two Tony's.

People lining up at Two Tony's

Of course, Thanksgiving was one of the most popular and crowded of the special holidays. One would expect Ted and Ruth Ann to make the Thanksgiving meal all inclusive with everything to make it the main "Event!" And it always was.

Celebrating Christmas at Two Tony's took place weeks before Christmas. Reservations for family gatherings began to come in weeks before Christmas. Businesses knew that to have a significant Christmas party, "We need to get our reservations in soon at Two Tony's." Weeks before December 25, Christmas decorations, cards, and Yuletide greetings began to appear along the walls, in the corners, and on the windows. Preparation for Christmas at Two Tony's was time consuming, hard work, and called for the complete cooperation of everyone.

There were many factors that made Two Tony's so successful. But one unique and noticeable addition really stood out. Every Christmas, Two Tony's displayed thirteen Christmas trees. Each one was large, reaching toward the ceiling and decorated according to a theme. The trees were strategically placed throughout the restaurant. Ted and Ruth Ann and the girls decorated each of the trees with their own personal touch and creativity.

One of the themes for the Christmas trees was sand dollars. On their family vacations to Florida, Ruth Ann and the girls would comb the beaches and collect sand-dollars. That was the making of that theme. And to add to the festive Christmas season, Two Tony's made it happen with the consistently large crowds that really ushered in a grand Christmas spirit.

Ruth Ann in front of one of the thirteen Christmas trees

But nothing rivaled the crowd and activity on Mother's Day. Two Tony's was packed and the line of people waiting to get in curled in a long line throughout the parking lot. The record crowd was on Mother's Day, 1988 with a little over three thousand persons coming to eat at Two Tony's.

"After twenty-eight years, almost seven days a week it became our lives. It was a great business for us. It fit our interests and our ambition. When we bought Two Tony's, we were excited to take on this new challenge because we saw so much we could do with Two Tony's. And we did just that. We put a lot of creativity, thought, and quality time in Two Tony's. Introducing new menu features, having an extensive and complete buffet selection, making the place comfortable and conducive to conversation, having the employees be happy and motivated, and making the place inviting and welcoming all were part of the image and reality of what we wanted Two Tony's to be. Bring the family and be comfortable."

Add to that, the fact that Two Tony's was also the place to work. For decades the Dairy Queen in Carmi was the place where the high school kids wanted to work. Working at the Dairy Queen, just a block away from the high school, was not only the place to work if you were in high school, but working at the Dairy Queen was also a rite of passage…you were somebody. It was the place to be, it was the place to work, it was the place to hang out. A long litany of kids from CTHS had the privilege of working at the Dairy Queen. The list of "graduates" who had the experience of working at the Dairy Queen, became identified as the "elite" of the young people of Carmi.

Two Tony's soon became one of the most favorite places in White County to work. Ted and Ruth Ann made the atmosphere attractive, welcoming, and enjoyable for young people and old alike. The kids said it was fun to work there. They gave credit to Ted and Ruth Ann for making it so. Of course, the sharp, attractive, and "I want one" uniforms were a big attraction for any young person who wanted to work at Two Tony's.

Ted and Ruth Ann made it work and made it work efficiently at Two Tony's. Each day there were so many contingencies that called for an understanding of running a business; important decisions had to be made about food reediness, relationships to employees and providing a good working environment, customers to be cared for, the interior and all the appointments had to be made welcoming, clean, and attractive. There had to be behind it all, a business knowledge that made things alive and of quality service. Ted and Ruth Ann were there from the first light of day until closing at night. How did they do it for twenty-eight years?

When a married couple makes it to seventy years, their friends and everyone who is acquainted with them, asks the question, "What is the secret to a marriage lasting so long?" One of their closest friends, without too much time to think of an answer, said, "Just off the top of my head, I can think of three reasons why Ted and Ruth Ann have made it through seventy years even with spending time with each other all day at Two Tony's. First, Ruth Ann had a way about her that made people think she was in charge. *The first reason people thought she was in charge, was because she made very good decisions. The second reason people thought she was in charge, was because she made sure things got done and got done right.* All the time she was at Two Tony's, she didn't sit around and hope for the best. She acted. *The third reason people thought she was in charge, was when difficult decisions had to be made, she didn't hesitate to act or step in and decide.*"

A good example is what took place when two Norris City kids were working at Two Tony's. Norris City is a town not far from Carmi and one of Carmi's opponents in sports. Sometimes the two boys from Norris City would make comments about the athletic teams at Carmi. Most of the time the comments weren't of a supportive or encouraging nature. Ruth Ann overheard them talking about Carmi sports in an uncomplimentary way, and told them "Stop this kind of talk or get out." From then on, they became good workers who kept their mouths shut.

Another example of Ruth Ann's quick action and decision making was a time at Two Tony's when a gentleman and four others came in for dinner from out of town. The men had been seated and the first one at the salad bar lit up a cigar and started through the line. Ruth Ann came up to him, took the cigar out of his mouth and told him, "There is no smoking here and especially in the food lines." After she took his cigar and started putting it out in an ash tray she was carrying, he took out another cigar and lit it up. Ruth Ann took that cigar out of his mouth also. She told him, "Didn't you hear what I said? If you do that again, you are out of here." He took another cigar out of his coat pocket and before he could light it up, she took him by the coat sleeve, marched him to the entrance and pushed him out the front door. The other men who were with him came to Ruth Ann and apologized to her. "We are sorry for what he did. He is always causing trouble someplace. We are glad you did what you did." He never tried to come back in, and his friends had their dinner with no further incidents.

Ted said that employee turnover was never an issue. Restaurants with forty employees in a small town usually face the task of dealing with turnover of employees. But, at Two Tony's, there was always a waiting list of those who wanted to wear the "one of a kind" uniform of Two Tony's.

Two things became very evident from those who worked there and wore the very distinctive uniforms. First, the uniforms the servers wore really drew attention, they enhanced the atmosphere of dining, highlighted the attitude and positive vibes of the workers, and by the common look of togetherness and unity, provided an atmosphere of order and greeting in contrast to the experience of disorder and uncertainty outside.

The second very important factor that made the dining experience so enjoyable, was Ruth Ann, the consummate host! Her presence, her greeting, her welcome, her attractiveness all became the first step in an unforgettable dining experience. Ruth Ann was asked if she attended any seminar or workshop or training event to learn how to be a host. She said no, she said she had learned on the job. I asked her what are the three most important roles for a host to perform at Two Tony's? She said, "First of all the host has to be pretty. Secondly, the host will have to know how to throw out drunks. Thirdly, the host has to exemplify kindness to everyone (except those who come in drunk) and assist the waitresses in insuring that the customer has a wonderful experience at Two Tony's."

The atmosphere, the ambiance, the comfort, the warm welcome were fashioned from the creative and sensitive skills of Ruth Ann and Ted. It is as if they asked themselves, "What can we do, what kind of atmosphere do we want Two Tony's to have, to make Two Tony's, the place to feel a sense of order, not chaos? To feel welcome and comfort? To really enhance the dining experience? What can we do to make Two Tony's conducive to being a healthy family experience? What can we do to make sure that owning Two Tony's and spending most of our time together at Two Tony's will be conducive to our marriage?"

There was and is only one answer to the question which has been asked to hundreds of young married couples who are going to spend time (a **lot** of time) working together. How can this venture turn out to be a "healthy experience" for this young couple? Ted answered for them both with a big smile and pointing directly at Ruth Ann as he said, "We were together in trials and rejoicing. But, thank God, more times of rejoicing. We did a good job working together and we became even better friends having had this experience."

Jan and Joan both worked at Two Tony's. Jan first began working at the Dairy Queen at age 15 and later began to work at Two Tony's. Jan was taken by the unique and attractive uniforms that really drew the attention of the customers and the enjoyment of the staff in wearing them.

Joan starting working at the age of thirteen. Because of her age she spent her first two years in the kitchen doing pots and pans, then she advanced to bus-boy, and other "grunt" work. Then she was advanced to the "line" by working to supply the buffet. Then, she too, became one of the servers and had the pleasure of wearing the Two Tony's uniform. With the training and supervision of Ruth Ann, the servers became the "focus" of attention, the symbol of "getting things done," and the "welcome to Two Tony's."

Jan Smith wearing Two Tony's waitress uniform

Joan Smith wearing Two Tony's waitress uniform

CHAPTER XII:

BEING PARENTS

《《 ♥ 》》

A. Young Parents

Jan made this observation about her parents, "Our dad and mom really created a major juxtaposition for us to deal with all our growing up lives. Dad was soft, not loud or aggressive, very intentional to get things done and get things done right. Very willing to make everybody feel good. I could get up in his lap and cuddle and tell him in a cooing kind of voice, 'Daddy, I really love you.' And then I would tell him what I wanted and of course, I got it. In most cases I got on his lap after mom said 'no.'"

I asked a question to Ted and Ruth Ann about the role they had early on as young parents...**really** young parents. As they thought about the question, they had to go back sixty plus years to think of that unique relationship to their daughters. Ruth Ann was the first to provide an answer. She said, slowly and with deep affection, "Ted was a great friend and even a greater father to our two girls." As if on cue, Ted followed with the same accolade, "Ruth Ann was not only a great friend but a great mother to our girls."

Joan adds to the description of the family encounters, "My dad never gave my dates a hard time when they came by to pick me up for a date. Being a big football star in college, my dad never played the role of a 'macho-stud' with any of my dates. He never stood over them to leer at them or threaten them. He never said a menacing word to them when he told them to get me home at a certain time."

Jan was quick to add that Ted never had any run-ins with her dates either. She said, "There were three reasons he didn't do any of those things. First of all, I only dated one boy from age fifteen on. His name was Eric and we dated all through high school and college and then we got married. Dad got to know him very well. Secondly, Eric was an athlete and respected and admired my dad a great deal. Eric knew more about my dad's reputation as a football player at Millikin than I did! Thirdly, Dad didn't intimidate anyone, especially any boy that came around. He never glared at a person in his life. He never stared anybody down. Dad and Eric had something in common that was very meaningful. Dad knew all about the idea of one girl for he was with mom, his "one girl" for over seventy years."

Joan said about the same thing. "My mom never gave my dates a hard time either. She didn't exactly make them feel comfortable all the time. Once, as my date and I were leaving the house for a date, she yelled for all the neighbors to hear, 'Joan, you keep your panties on.'"

I asked Ted, "What was the biggest disappointment you experienced as a dad to your two girls?" I expected him to say something his daughters neglected which turned out to be a disappointment to him. Or, he might mention they did something that didn't enhance their relationship with mom and dad. Or, he was disappointed they missed the opportunity to participate in a family experience that they had planned. I expected him to mull my question over in his mind, hem and haw around, and finally stammer something about their high school years.

I didn't expect him to take the blame for the biggest disappointment he might mention. I didn't expect him to make the claim he was the reason for the disappointment. He became silent and just stared at the floor as he was really thinking on this one. I got the impression he had dealt with this question before. After a long pause, he gave a distinct and clearly articulated answer, choking back tears, he said, "The biggest disappointment I had as a parent, (here was the struggle at this point to keep the tears from interrupting what he was going to say) was that during the time we owned Two Tony's, I didn't spend more time with the girls."

As he was reflecting on the disappointment, tears welled up in his eyes. He became very silent. The disappointment he described was clearly understood. In that moment I learned a great deal about the measure of the man. It was not like Ted Smith to put the blame on someone else when it was his responsibility. If there were accolades to pass out, he did that thoughtfully taking no credit for himself. And, if there was disappointment to identify, he always looked inward at himself, he didn't blame anyone.

And Ruth Ann's answer to the same question was a mirror of what Ted said. "What was your biggest disappointment at being a mom to your two girls?" Immediately, without putting a lot of thought to my question, she answered, "That is easy. My biggest disappointment at being a mom to those two girls is that they were much smarter than me. There were so many things I wanted to teach them, show them, and discuss with them. Some things only a mother could do. But they were always a step ahead of me. My biggest disappointment was that I was never able to reach way down and touch them where we could have had another level of conversation."

Jan had mentioned that, "My parents never raised their voices at each other. I can't remember a time when they yelled in anger or frustration. They just never did. The only time that I can remember when one of them got angry was the day we went to Evansville to pick out my wedding dress. Mom and I were in back of the store looking at dresses. We picked out two that we were going to consider. Mom wanted a particular one and I wanted another one. We both were not willing to bend. So, I asked mom if dad could come in a see which one he wanted. Dad came in the dressing room and mom told him our dilemma. He said, 'It is Jan's wedding, let her pick out her own dress.' Dad turned around and went back to his chair to continue to wait until we were done. It was clear which dress I would get.

We made our selection, got dad, and got in the car to come home. Mom never said a word all the way home. She was angry, but she never said a word. When we got to Carmi we were stopped at the light in front of the Baptist Church. We were several blocks from home. Mom was in the backseat. When the light changed and dad started down the street, mom said 'Stop the car, please.' Dad stopped the car; she got out and walked the rest of the way home.

"We got home and were sitting in the living room waiting for mom to walk in. We heard her when she got to the front porch. She came in and didn't say a word. She went to the bedroom and quietly closed the door. We knew she was angry because we knew which dress she wanted me to buy and we knew what her silence meant and her decision to walk home.

"After a couple of days of being cordial and watching what we said and how we said it, dad and I overheard her on the phone tell a friend how much she liked my wedding dress. She would tell anyone who would listen, how much she liked the wedding dress. When someone would come to the house to inquire about the wedding dress, she would say, 'Just look at this dress. Isn't it the most beautiful thing you have ever seen?"

Ruth Ann was great at making sure everything was done efficiently and impressively. As Terri, one of their friends said, "Everything that Ruth Ann did, especially what she would do for someone else, it was over the top. I had prepared a very special tea party for my daughter's fourth birthday. I even ordered special plates for the occasion. The special plates didn't come in time for the party and I was very upset. I told Ruth Ann, and she brought over some very special plates that were over one hundred years old. I told her these were four-year-old girls, the plates may be broken to pieces." She said, "So what?"

B. The First Wedding

Jan said, "My wedding was an occasion that was over the top. The reception and the whole event were a great feat that mom had put together. And it was all done out of great love that my mother had for all of us. Everything, the wedding ceremony and the reception afterwards, had her personal hand and touch to make it all perfect. She and dad eloped and she never had the kind of wedding I had. And she was going to make sure I had everything she wanted it to be.

"The reception was another one of her 'over the top' great events. Dad also had a lot to do with that. It was to be the traditional wedding reception. It was to last the usual length of about two hours. It was held at Two Tony's and Ted had closed the restaurant early and filled the serving lines with all kinds of tasty appetizers, delicacies to satisfy most tastes, and appointed treats that spelled success. When the two hours ticked on the clock, everyone, including a few who came off the street, were having a great time. The noise even seemed to hit a crescendo and no one was ready to leave or even thought about heading for the door."

It was more than a wedding reception; it was a community "event." It was held on Thanksgiving and that added to the festival-like atmosphere and the celebratory mood that everyone felt. Some folks must have come off the streets of Carmi to be a part of this grand time. Ruth Ann estimates the reception crowd to be about seven hundred friends, family, and assorted guests.

The time seemed to pass away quickly and the band which had been hired by Ted, was about to start packing up to leave. With the band packing up, Ted saw the possibilities of the night's activity coming to an end. Seeing he had to act fast, he approached the band leader and said, "If you would stay another hour, I will give you two hundred dollars." The band leader looked at the band for a nod of approval and they all nodded "yes." So, the band played on.

Ted and Ruth Ann's brother saw the need to "juice up" the punch bowl. Ted knew the owner of the liquor store across the street, Jimmy Gaines. But it was closed. Ted called him and told him of the need. "Would you meet me at your store? It would really be a big help to us." "Sure, I would be glad to." Ted picked up several cases of a variety of drinks.

To add to the festivities, Ruth Ann's brother, Van Ward, had his son go to their house and get all the booze they had and bring it to the reception. When his son got back to the reception with his "contribution" he poured some of it (quite a bit) in the punch bowl. The son, not old enough to know better, hung around the punch bowl and needed to be assisted away.

By this time, the band has done their extra hour. They began to get ready to pack up a second time. A second time Ted approached them and said, "We are just getting warmed up in here. We hate to see you go. Would you stay another hour for another two hundred dollars? Again, the band leader looked for a nod of approval from the band and they all nodded "yes." So, the band played on.

After that additional hour was over, the punch bowl was getting dry, the drinks were down to empty bottles, and the band had been visiting the punch bowl. As they were finally getting packed up leave the third time and feeling the "joy" of the punch bowl, they told Ted, "If you want us to stay another hour it won't cost a cent, just keep the punch bowl filled. We don't give a shit if we are here all night." Ted told them that the end had finally come and how much everyone appreciated their contribution to a memorable night.

The bride and groom had made their exit, and people were saying their good byes. Things got awfully quiet. After everyone was gone, Ted and Ruth Ann sat down with her brother, had a short "night-cap" and reveled in having hosted one of the best wedding receptions in the history of Carmi and Maunie.

C. Reflections on Home

Jan said, "There are all kinds of memories we have of mom and dad while we were growing up. One of the most important and most wonderful was the fifteenth birthday party my mom gave me. It was a big affair. It was in October, and we had a Halloween theme. It was an unforgettable Halloween party with chili and all the trimmings. Mom even had a special event for us. Mrs. Ragsdale came as a fortune teller. That was a very special gift that mom gave me. The whole birthday party was a wonderful gift of love. She gave Joan and me birthday parties we will never forget.

"The birthday parties were not like any family would have except ours. Mom, in her creative and generous display of 'let's have a good time,' made it happen." From being just preschoolers on, the birthday party was structured around the two sisters sitting in chairs back-to-back with the birthday girl receiving her gifts all wrapped and ready to be opened. The other sister had the same gifts but they were not wrapped, just in a bag. The birthday girl opened her gifts, one by one and the other sister retrieved a gift from her bag. This birthday ritual went on until about junior high then it slowly came to an end. When they were sixteen, the gifts were no longer several gift-wrapped items, but cars.

It was mentioned that Ruth Ann was great at reminiscing, of putting a picture together of some significant experience. "She reveled in past occasions and retelling them. She would bring something up that took place in my life or our family's life and she would bring to life the picture of the experience. I couldn't remember any of it, but she would relive it in such a wonderful way; the things that were said, the things that were done, who was there, and what the total experience was for everyone."

Jan added to that collage of memories that Ted had a hand in making possible. She told about the time she came home from getting her hair cut. "It was a disaster and I came home and went to the basement and just started crying. I was so upset and discouraged. Dad asked mom what the trouble was. She said, 'She is very upset about her hair cut. She says when she goes to school the kids will laugh and point at her.'"

So, Ted went down to the basement and asked her what the trouble was. "Look at my hair! The kids are all going to laugh at me." "All dad said was, 'Nobody will notice.' That is all he said. And he went back upstairs. I couldn't believe he didn't care. That is all he said, "Nobody will notice." At school the next day, no one noticed."

When you see pictures of your dad and mom in their high school yearbooks, what do you think, what comes to your mind, as you really tune in at those pictures? Jan said, "I have done that often and I think how young they were. And here they are getting married, having a baby, moving to a new town away from all they know and love, everything so unfamiliar. I think of all that mom had to consider as a sixteen-year-old girl, and all the responsibilities she must now assume."

Of course, looking at the sports area of the yearbooks, you see a lot of pictures of Ted Smith. When the daughters were asked if they were aware of their dad's sports reputation, they said he seldom talked about it. They said, "If it weren't for some of the boys at school or some of dad's friends, we would never have known he was a star football player in high school and college. We never heard dad talk about himself as a star athlete. He was not about that. He seldom talked about his exploits in sports. *He would do nothing or say anything that would distance himself from mom.*"

"In spite of her many responsibilities and always being busy as a young mother, she always had special bits of advice that only a young mother could give…at least OUR mother. And her advice was

107

not always the predictable and expected advice that mothers give their daughters. For instance, I consider the best advice I ever got from mom was, 'Always look pretty.' Then she would follow that with, 'Be sure to make your bed.'"

One memory that will stand out with the girls is centered on the phone call Ruth Ann made to the high school to tell the girls to come home. She left a message with the administrative office staff to tell the girls to come home. Such a call from a parent has an alarming quality about it. The thought as to why such a call from a parent is made has an urgency about it. Such a call is usually bad news and sometimes critical for the family. The girls got in Jan's car and hurried home, wondering what could be the issue. They quickly entered the house and immediately saw Ruth Ann waiting for them. "You girls didn't make your beds. Now get up there and take care of it."

Never before, in the experience of secondary education, in the history of the world, has a mother called the school to have her kid or kids come home to make their bed or beds. When the girls were told why they were called home, they looked at each other in disbelief. Once the shock had worn off, Joan mumbled to Jan "Mom called us home for this?"

It is hard to imagine that a young father with young daughters would be entertaining the notion of Living Will, Power of Attorney, and the question of Executor. But Ted was very intentional about making those plans and having them documented. He made Jan executor, because she is the oldest. To make sure that preparation and execution of the legal matter was complete and fulfilled, he spoke to Joan. "I want you to know that since Jan is the oldest, it only makes sense that she would be the executor of our last will and testament. And there will be no surprises when that time comes. You both will receive 50%. Both equal. The paper work is done and you girls will not have to do any legal maneuvering to take care of details after we are gone.

The girls said that the question about college after high school was non-negotiable. "You girls are going to college, that is an absolute. "The process of choosing which college to attend became *a very complex process.* It was to be a significant and well thought out decision. The family took this major hurdle very seriously. There was a *four-step evaluative procedure* that, followed *with professional counsel,* would determine where we would go. The process we followed to select a college for us was defined by the following four criteria;

1. Academic reputation
2. Consider area of major study....expertise in the area.
3. Extra curriculum expectations.
4. Scholarship opportunity."

This complicated academic formulated process, although followed by the book, was described in detail by Jan: "Erick chose Eastern, I went where he went, Joan wanted to go where I went, and her boyfriend wanted to go where she went. So, we all ended up at Eastern Illinois University in Charleston, Illinois."

The four-step process, as outlined above, was a very complex and detailed endeavor which had the endorsement and recommendations of Harvard, Yale, and Stanford. For this *very difficult and serious mental consideration*, the Smith girls made a good choice.

CHAPTER XIV:

THE FAMILY TAKES SHAPE

A. Talking to Jan

The biggest challenge facing Ted and Ruth Ann was telling Jan she was born five months after they got married. That was probably the most anxious of any issue facing this young married couple. The number one worry for Ruth Ann, was telling Ted "I am pregnant." Then, the worry is telling their parents. Then once Ted and Ruth Ann get married, their worry is the anticipated confrontation of telling Jan she was born just a few months after they were married.

That was the worry, the anxious thoughts that Ted and Ruth Ann dealt with for the first couple of years. The questions they raised and had to consider were; "How old should she be before we tell her? How will we tell her? Who will tell her, or will it be both of us? Where would be the best place to tell her? If we don't tell her and she finds out accidently, then do we really have a problem?"

Soon after Ted and Ruth Ann moved back to Carmi, and the girls were in middle school, they decided that would be the time to tell her. It was decided that Ted would tell her. Ted and Ruth Ann thoughtfully considered what they would say.

They tried to figure what would be the best time to tell her and how to fashion the best and most comfortable circumstances. Should we do it at home with the TV off and no one else around? Downtown at Werly's? Pick her up at school and go for a drive? It was decided that Ted would tell her after he picked her up from school. While driving home, he would determine when and how to tell her. Then he would try to tell her the message that he and Ruth Ann felt about their love for Jan. He wanted to let her know that she was one of the most important aspects of their married lives. The message he wanted her to know, was that she became a wonderful expression of their love for each other. That she was planned, but she just came early.

Ted began the conversation with, "Everything that took place after your mom told me she was pregnant, was just what we had planned to do all along. You did not force us to get married. We planned to anyhow. You did not force us to leave Carmi and move to Decatur. We planned to anyhow. The only change you brought about was we just did all we had to do, sooner. And that turned out to be a blessing for us. You were the blessing and you enabled us to have love at the center of our family. You not only made our family a wonderful experience, you were the essential that made us the family we became. The four of us became one all bound in love. The four of us became linked as one because of our love for each other. You were truly God's gift to us. We wouldn't want it any other way."

Jan said, "I guess dad was surprised that I didn't get upset or looked like I had just been told something shocking. I told him that I had read in the paper, the article about him coming to Carmi to sell life insurance. In the article it mentioned when you and mom were married. Then I put my birthdate in the equation and came to the conclusion that I was born not long after you were married. But I appreciate you telling me.

I think dad felt a great deal of relief."

Few families have such a vast array of meaningful, treasured, memorable, and joyful experiences as what Ted and Ruth Ann fashioned to take place in their family. And then later, Jan and Joan fashioned their own contributions that became a litany of blessings to the whole family; two daughters who made sure their parents knew of their love for them; two daughters who nurtured a strong tie to their parents which gained their trust, two daughters who lived their lives in a way that gained respect from their parents.

One of the important tools or opportunities that made that vast array of meaningful, treasured, memorable, and joyful experiences take place in this family, was the time spent as a family at Barkley Lake. They had a trailer house and a boat in which they had weekends of sharing time together.

They spent their time laughing, talking with and over each other, eating, fishing, boating, and absorbing the sun. But there was work to be done at the site. They had to maintain the trees and then all that one has to do for clean-up when so many trees are around.

Barkley Lake has been a symbol, a point of entry, a place that had special meaning to the family of four that assured them of their importance to each other. Most families don't have such an "anchor" that gives them a sense of security, stability, and a place to nurture family bonds. The Smith family had the place where they could go to charge their batteries, put depth to their relationship, and reaffirm their place with each other.

One would think, and many did, that Jan and Joan were twins. Some joked that they were of the notion the sisters were clones. One of their friends made the observation that Jan and Joan saw in their mother and father the "oneness" that they were on track to be the same. Ruth Ann said that as young girls they would sometimes dress the same and people did think of them as twins.

112

The fact is that Jan and Joan had their own expressions of being unique individuals. Jan was more the academician. Joan says of her sister, "Jan was the student. Dad and Mom hardly ever had to tell her to study or worry about her grades. She made straight A's. I didn't struggle, but I was not the student she was."

But the dominant thought and comment that many made toward Jan and Joan, was that they were "good girls." I mentioned to Ruth Ann that those were the words I heard so often, Her response? "They were damn good girls!" So, I asked them, "What is meant when people say you were "good girls?" They were quick to answer; "We learned to toe the line. We wanted our parents to be proud of us. We didn't want them to be angry at us. When mom told us to do something, we did it. It was important to us that we would please them.'" One of Ruth Ann's good friends said that people would mention how good the girls were. She said, "They were good girls because Ted and Ruth Ann were always there for them for all the school activities in which they took part. They had this confidence that comes when they knew they were loved so much. And, I will tell you something else that made them good girls, THEY KNEW THE RULES THEIR MOM AND DAD LAID OUT FOR THEM!"

B. The Second Wedding

Although the girls were close in age, they were also close because they found security in each other. That was necessary because, as Jan said, "We moved around often when we were young and we depended on each other to feel less lonely."

But the differences in the girls was noticeable. The weddings were especially symbolic of the differences between the sisters. Jan invited five hundred to her wedding. If someone who did not get an invitation and they wanted to come, they would call and say, "We never received an invitation to your wedding. It must have gotten lost in the mail. We really would like to come but we don't want to impose." Jan would reply, "I am very sorry you didn't get an invitation; it must have been my error. I am so sorry and would be more than happy to have you come. I hope you will be able to make it."

Joan invited fifty people. A friend of Ruth Ann who did not get an invitation, did call and talked to Ruth Ann and said, "Ruth Ann, I didn't get an invitation to Joan's wedding. I just wanted to call and make sure it would be OK if I came." Ruth Ann said, "Just a minute, I will let you talk to Joan." When Joan took the phone, the caller repeated her request. "Hi, Joan, I didn't get an invitation to your wedding and I just wanted to let you know how much I would like to be there." Joan said, "We just invited fifty people and that's all we invited to attend." Then she handed the phone back to her mom.

C. Cars For The Sixteenth Birthdays

When it came time for the sixteenth birthday of each girl, the difference became more obvious. Jan was given a new Ford Mustang. Ted ordered it from the local Ford dealer. When it came in it was placed in the show room wrapped with a big bow. When her Dad got the phone call that it was in, he told Jan that she could go down to the dealership and pick it up. Eric accompanied her to the dealership and they reveled in the excitement of the occasion.

She couldn't wait to take it out to show it off. The celebration had reached its height as Jan made use of the horn when she saw her friends. It was a "look at what I just got for my birthday!" Eric and Jan took the car out toward Enfield and went off the main road to see more completely how it felt. Unknown to them was that the road had just been oiled! The Ford Mustang hit the road as only a sixteen-year-old girl could make it go. Suddenly, they realized what was happening. For the first time in their experience, they had hit a newly oiled road.

They knew this was bad. They knew it was VERY BAD especially with a new Ford Mustang. "Why couldn't we have just drove it in the rain? Why not just mud? Why not just dust? No, the real test would be to drive through a freshly oiled road which was being used by oil field trucks and grain trucks from the farms. It was not to be a test road for a brand-new Ford Mustang."

They drove back home to show Ted what had happened. The problem was that the new Ford Mustang was to be in the Annual Corn Day parade the next day!

What to do! As soon as they got home, they (all of them) began to clean it up.

At Joan's sixteenth birthday, Ted asked her what kind of car she wanted. She said she did not want a car. "But this is special, it is your sixteenth birthday." What better comment could a dad make? For days Joan said she just was not interested. Finally, he did persuade her to go with him to just look around at cars in the dealership lots.

The more they looked around, the more she saw cars that looked too much like her dad's. At each place a sales person would give a very inviting pitch and Joan's response was very lukewarm or a response that conveyed, "not interested." Ted kept trying to encourage her. "Look at this one, honey. This color is just what a college student would want." After taking more time looking around, Joan became more convinced she did not want a car and the more she convinced her dad his quest was a losing battle. Ted became very discouraged that he couldn't convince her to get a car.

But then, about three months after her sixteenth birthday, Joan made the suggestion to her dad that she was having second thoughts about having a car. It was like saying, "I know it is three months since I turned sixteen, but does the offer still stand on getting a new car?"

"Sure, it does. It will still be your sixteenth birthday gift from your mom and me. What kind of car do you want?" "A Corvette." Ted said something to the effect of, "When you change your mind, you really change it." One of the reasons she said she didn't want a car was that they only lived a half block from the school. But the Corvette would make it just fine.

Joan had the Corvette when she went to college. There were times when it was just the car to have. Who is not impressed by a Corvette? But it could only seat two people. "There would be times when I need to haul "stuff" back and forth from school to home. Also, I may want to give a ride home to some of my friends who live down here. Then I will have to take them back to Charleston and haul more stuff back to school. So, what to do? I will ask Dad if he will trade me his car for mine. He said, 'OK, because I know you women have to have your 'stuff.'"

CHAPTER XV:

"THE COUPLE THAT RACES TOGETHER, STAYS TOGETHER"

It is usually very simple to identify the roles a couple takes when they are into harness racing. The man, husband, boyfriend is usually the jockey, driver, owner of the horse, trainer, even so-called-veterinarian, and in general, has control over the horse. The wife, or girlfriend, or significant other will just be a pretty face who stands off to the side at the winner's circle. She will probably be wearing a beautiful elegant hat that will enhance the winner's circle. The hat will not match the jockey/driver silks, but that is not expected. She will not be interviewed but she will hold a place of attention that will rival the winning horse. She is just told to smile and leave the race-track talk to the owner/driver.

As husband and wife, Ted and Ruth Ann were equally involved in harness racing. It was a very time-consuming sport and costly. But Ted and Ruth Ann immersed themselves in racing in such a way, that we on the outside have a hard time determining who does the leading, who was in charge, Ted or Ruth Ann.

The typical racing couple, Ted and Ruth Ann *were not*. One of them took the initiative to get most everything ready and everything in its place. Neither one waited for the other to say, "Go." The litany of what to do, was familiar to each of them, and they did it. "Make sure we have ample resources stored and ready for our investments.

Is the barn or stables prepared to care for our vested interests? What is the field like for today's race? Is that kid farmer from Ft. Branch, Indiana still clamoring about a rough track? Tell him to just go home. Everybody here, just wants to race. I will get the buckets and brushes ready and have them handy. I will make sure the stable master is ready for the post-race rubdown. I will make sure our brushes and tack are available and ready."

That is what Ruth Ann said she would be doing. Ted? He said, "I will make sure the racing silks are duly administered. I will do my stretching early on and take my place in the seat. Then we are ready to go. Ruth Ann will take care of all the necessary preparations."

Ted and Ruth Ann in a horse race

But some of the women who are part of a racing team only dress for the occasion. Ruth Ann dresses for the occasion, but she has on her work boots, not the fashionable cowgirl boots from Ralph's in Dallas, Texas. She has work gloves, not fashioned glamor gloves from Shapiro's in Los Angeles. She wears a blazer that does not convey the line of DeBussie Del Mar, but a blazer (denim jacket) that conveys THE CARMI RACING TEAM from White County, Illinois on the back. She has on jeans (not designer slacks from Macy's) with an apron to keep the horse food supplement liquid from staining her jeans.

When one expected to see "R. A. Bugger" take his place at the starting line, they would see Ruth Ann take her time in getting him in the proper "spot." Because Ruth Ann was so familiar with R. J. Bugger's "feel" as to where to "fit" at the starting line, she let him lead her. After he looked over some of the positions, he made his stand when he saw his spot. And, there was no doubt when he felt he had found his spot.

Then, after all the preliminaries are over and Ruth Ann has done her pre-race chores, we are ready for "They're off!"

Ruth Ann usually takes the most advantageous place in the stands. She will have three time watches, two split time watches, and an official oval route time piece. She will find a place where the timers will not be affected by some spectator.

In a particular race in St. Louis, Ruth Ann found herself seated in front of a contingent of black racing fans. She overheard them go through their ritual of picking a horse for each race. When R. J. Bugger was paraded and introduced, one would have thought that Joe Louis had been introduced. The blacks behind Ruth Ann began their verbal selection process. "There he is!" they yelled, as they saw R. J. Bugger find his spot in the lineup. "He is our main man! Nobody can hold him. He will make short work of all those other horses."

As the race progressed, R. J. Bugger won hands down. The racing fans behind Ruth Ann erupted in yells and shouts.

But Ruth Ann did not engage her fans who just cleaned up with R. J. Bugger. She had a burning desire to tell them, "I understand you wagered on R. J. Bugger. I own him. He is mine. My husband is the driver." But she just had a smile as if to tell them, "Don't spend all your winnings in one place."

How does a person start getting involved in harness racing? Surely there has to be a "training/indoctrination/session" to become acquainted with the truck-load of terms and glossary of phrases used in the sport. No sport has a more complex and larger litany of terms with which to become acquainted than harness racing.

How about getting acquainted with the jargon that refers just to the horses? Let's start with the simple ones, like *WEANLING* which means, *"A foal that is less than one year old that has been separated from its DAM."* Or, *DAM* which means *"The mother of a horse." MARE, a female horse four years or older, FILLY, a female horse four years old or younger, FOAL, a newborn horse under one year old, GELDING, a neutered male horse of any age, MAIDEN, a horse who has never won a race with a purse, IN FOAL, a pregnant mare, FREE-LEGGED, a pacer which races without wearing hopples.*

And then, there are all the eighty-three other terms that one has to learn to be a driver or owner of a harness racer. But Ted and Ruth Ann did it. They did it so well that their competitors often looked askance at their preparation prior to each race. "What are they doing to place so well in all these races? For instance, at one track Ted and Ruth Ann won eight races in a row. The seasoned and experienced racers began to pay attention to these "rookies." If it was a golf match, they would check the ball to see if it is "legal." If it was baseball, they would check the bat to see if it has been "doctored."

But Ted and Ruth Ann weren't always in the winner's circle. At one track Ted was anxious to see what his horse could do. It was a lightning rod field with a line-up of quality racers, just the right conditions to see how the horse could perform. The trainer noticed a slight swelling on the front left knee of the horse. The vet was called in and he simply gave the horse a shot in the knee. Nothing was seriously wrong and the shot would simply take care of the swelling.

But suddenly the horse began to lower his head, stumble around in the stall, and lose the ability to stand steady. The veterinarian checked his vial for the vaccination and found it was not the intended medicine, but a tranquilizer! The horse was not able to race that evening and never was able to race again.

The loss of the horse was a great loss to Ted and Ruth Ann. Not only was the loss in money but the horse had become a favorite and it was considered a long-term investment for Ted and Ruth Ann. No suit was filed against the vet. He was a good friend of Ted and Ruth Ann and the incident was considered a very unfortunate accident.

Why did Ted and Ruth Ann get so attracted to harness racing and involved in such a way that racing became a special favorite activity in their lives? What got their attention? Ted's brother from Texas came up for a visit and spent a lot of time at the horse stables at the White County Fair grounds. Ted joined him and became quite fascinated by the attention given the horses. He became more attached as he watched the drivers take the horses out on the track to practice. Then he could feel the power in the presence and size of the noise, the flash of excitement in the horse's anticipation, and imagined the flow of energy as the starter's flag was first sighted. Ted got hooked.

How in the world did Ted and Ruth Ann get involved in such a way, that the winner's circle would be familiar to them? How long did it take for Ted to take over the driver's seat and be his own driver? In two weeks, Ted asked the one who should know, Charles Cleveland, "What do I do if I want to race?" "Just take a horse out for a few laps and see if it suits you." In just a short time, less than two weeks, Ted said, "This is it. I can do this. And I did."

"That was in 1978. For about twenty years Ruth Ann and I raced and did a great job. We had some wonderful horses and had a very good time. It was a very rewarding experience. A friend of mine who is in the achives of racing locally, once told me that my winning record is one of the best in Illinois harness racing. Ruth Ann and I had some really good horses.

"On one occasion we were down in Henderson, Kentucky for a race. I did well that race at Riverside Downs. There were several people there who were acquainted with harness racing and were impressed by my horse. Some were out of state. Three gentlemen from New Jersey came to our stall and began to talk to us. They were very complimentary about our horse and asked if we would be willing to sell him. We told them no, but they showed a genuine interest and continued their conversation with us. In just a few minutes I asked them what they would pay for my horse. They made an offer, and we took it.

"A few weeks later, I received a call from one of the men who bought the horse. He said, 'We can't get him to do anything. He won't run like we know he can. He just doesn't want to work or run. Can you help us out?'

"I told him that he likes the hobbles to be a certain length. And he has to have his right front hoof lifted a bit. I asked where they put the hobbles on him. If you put them at medium length that might be the problem. And check the padding on his right front hoof. About two months later they called again from New Jersey and said, 'We made the adjustments you suggested and out of the last six races, he has won the last four and place second in two others. He has already paid for himself.'"

There are all kinds of idiosyncracies that these horses have, with which a driver or trainer has to deal. One of the most successful horses that Ted and Ruth Ann owned, was T.J. Whisper. T. J. Whisper won several races and it was only after he did not find himself in the winner's circle, that Ted and Ruth Ann found his "Achilles heel."

If he wasn't in the lead, he just gave up. He had to be in front. It is a condition that is not too common with race horses, but it is still a problem to deal with if it happens to be your horse. The solution? Make sure he starts out in front. When the gate is opened, full throttle. Concentrate on the starter's flag, his arm, and when he moves, full throttle. The curve is just forty yards away and it is a prescription for mayhem to charge to that narrow curve to be the first one at the rail. But T. J. Whisper had to charge to the lead."

One of the biggest lessons Ted learned during his racing horses was when someone asked about a horse winning and what was the reason for his win that day. Ted said, "He didn't win today, he won this past week when we trained. That was the case with Regal Lee. Regal Lee won twelve out of sixteen races. Each win was due to his training the weeks before the race."

Ted and Ruth Ann were into the racing phase of their lives while they were owners of Two Tony's. Two Tony's was closed Monday and Tuesday so those two days became race days for Ted and Ruth Ann.

But few people realize the role that Ruth Ann had in this venture. Did she just hold back and not make her presence known? Did she just go along and let Ted do all the planning and preparation? Or, did she take charge once in a while. At one such opportunity, she let it be known that she still had a say and was going let it be known. At one showing of a grand display of a horse, she took the opportunity to exercise her right to be in charge.

A beautiful filly horse was brought in the show-case arena and trotted around. The horse was a selected horse for this special sale. As the horse was being led into the arena, it bolted from the handler. All of a sudden, the horse broke and ran out of the arena. Several persons took off from the arena to catch the runaway filly. The crowd began to concentrate on the runaway filly.

Many in the crowd that witnessed the filly taking off, began to place bets on whether the horse would return or not. The announcer, hearing the wagers being made, said to the crowd, "If she returns, who wants to buy her?" She was the only horse in the sale. Ruth Ann shouted to the auctioneer, "I will take her." "Sold!" Ruth Ann now had a horse. When the horse was finally found and returned to the arena, it was announced that Ruth Ann had won the "bet" and now owned the runaway horse. She told Ted, who was not at the sale, that she had bought him. He had a bewildered look on his face and he said, "You did what?"

CHAPTER XVI:

SELLING TWO TONY'S

O ne would think that after owning a business for twenty-eight years, it would be an anxiety-provoking event to consider selling it. It would be something that would take a lot of thinking. Is it really the best move? Is it really the best time? What will we do with ourselves without the routine we have had all these years? Are we making the right move?

The process of selling Two Tony's did not follow the usual practice of a business being sold. The machinery started moving when Ruth Ann and Ted came home after another day and night of working at Two Tony's. Ruth Ann went to the bedroom and began to wind down from working all day. She said to Ted, "I am getting tired of this. After all these years, I am really tired of this." Ted listened and said he felt the same way. The common denominator that Ruth Ann came out with; "Too much restaurant. From 6 AM to 10 PM."

Ted said that he would go in to see Tom Daniels and Bill Foster in the morning. They were in the oil field drilling business. They were good friends with Ted. They played golf together and knew each other for several years. Their office was downtown on the second floor of the First National Bank building. The next morning, Ted walked into their office. They were both sitting at their desks. Ted said, as he walked into their office, "they had the funniest looks on their faces."

They looked at each other as if they were surprised to see Ted. They told Ted that they were just talking about him.

Ted told them, "Well, I don't know what you were talking about, but I just came by to see if you would be interested in buying Two Tony's. Maybe Two Tony's is something your nephew Stan would want to take over."

They responded that they would be interested and they asked Ted what he was asking for it. Ted told them, "Here is the asking price. But I want to tell you, this is the asking price today, tomorrow it will be different. Also, I want you to know that I don't want a down payment and then you pay monthly payments. I want it paid in full now."

They said they would make some phone calls today. Immediately they called Sam, Stan's brother, who is an attorney in Evansville. They talked to all those they needed to make the purchase and Stan's brother would draw up the sales contract.

In twenty-four hours, Ted and Ruth Ann had sold Two Tony's. Stan ran it for seven years. At the time of the sale, Ted asked Stan if he would like him to stay on to help him and his new business staff get acquainted and help in the transition.

Stan did not take Ted up on his offer. He had his own style of leadership and method of running the restaurant. He wanted to establish his own brand of the food served and his way of serving it. He did want the forty employees to stay and continue working. Most of them gladly stayed.

But Stan's style of ownership as it related to the employees was much different from Ted and Ruth Ann's. Ted and Ruth Ann fashioned their relationship to their employees much different from Stan. They created an atmosphere and work environment that resembled a "family" operation. They did not relish being "boss" and did not expect the servers and cooks and service employees to "toe the line" or feel pressured. In such a work-place, the rate of turnover was minimal. Two Tony's was the place to work. People, especially the young people, readily filled out the application to work at Two Tony's. The reason was very clear – Ted and Ruth Ann.

On the other hand, Stan's style of being the boss was very different. His style had expectations that were not so much about being efficient, but demanding. His relationship to the staff was less working together, but rather, "get the work done and do it now." His way of putting the work place in order by suggestion and assistance, was more by ordering and insistence.

Shortly after Stan took over as owner, his style of being boss, created a crisis one Sunday after the food lines were in place. The hot food line was prepared and ready and the cold line, the salad line, was prepared and ready. But he had said something to some of the employees that did not set well with several of them. On that Sunday, the busiest day for a first-class buffet, the worst time for conflict in a restaurant, took place. The whole crew of Two Tony's restaurant, walked out. Stan had crossed the line.

Two Tony's was closed on Monday and Tuesday. It was a good thing. With the staff walking out on Sunday, it took at least two days to get a staff in place to carry on the business. Stan's aunt was called upon to salvage the direction and operation of Two Tony's. She was a cook at an elementary school and took over the effort to "re-open" the restaurant. The restaurant opened on Wednesday of that week. His aunt put things in order and did a lot in getting new employees to work.

After seven years of owning and managing Two Tony's, Stan faced another crisis. Two Tony's caught on fire. The fire started in the kitchen above the hood which was over the stove. Flames began to really engulf the back of the restaurant and completely overtook the kitchen. At two o'clock in the morning, people driving by could see the flames. The fire department was called and the fire was finally contained but only after the back and the kitchen area was completely ruined. The good thing was that the front of the store, the dining rooms, were untouched. Yet, the insurance company settled the claim of total destruction. There was no official review of the claim but it was pointed out to me that questions still are raised as to the credibility of the claim.

Selling Two Tony's was the last major decision in our lives. The night Ruth Ann said, 'I am really tired of this' that was a moment that put us in a new and different direction for the rest of our lives. But we were ready to sell! Oh, we made a good living. We hated to see that end. And, it was a great place to meet people and have a good time with them. We knew we were going to miss that routine we had for twenty-eight years. But, as I said before, we were ready to sell. It was time and we knew it."

Ted and Ruth Ann

CHAPTER XVII:

EXTRAORDINARY, EXCEPTIONAL

Two factors define the success of the marriage of Ted and Ruth Ann Smith. First of all, they were always working, organizing, planning, and making sure things got done. Their friends always said, "They had good work ethics."

The second factor, and probably the most important, quality of their marriage is the fact that Ted and Ruth Ann are crazy about each other. It has been said by so many who know them, "When you see one, you see the other. They are inseparable." Another friend said, "It is not that they don't like being apart from each other, they like being with each other." Joan made the observation that "We could tell as we heard them, saw them, experienced their presence, but above all, we FELT they cared for each other."

Marty Hinshelwood (Gilpin) said that she and her close friends, Barbara, Nancy, and Ruth Ann had planned to have a reunion after they were out of college. They had planned to meet in Idaho and have a reunion. It was mentioned, in the planning, that just the four of them would get together. Ruth Ann said, as they were making their plans, "Teddy will have to come." That is when the other three knew for sure that Ted and Ruth Ann were inseparable. As they learned, "You see one, you see the other. They are always together." "I won't come without Ted." That was a statement etched in concrete. So, the husbands joined in that reunion and all the rest.

What made it work for seventy years? One other friend said, "They really know how to give and take. With them, no one gets put down and no one insists on their own way."

I asked Ted to what he attributes their success as a couple and as a family. He thought for a few moments and as tears welled up in his eyes he said, "It is all because of her. She has sacrificed so much. She has given so much. So, we made it due to Ruth Ann and the Lord."

As he quietly sat and looked ahead with a look of wanting to add more to such an important point, he said, "One of the most important aspects of our relationship and that which really defines our success as a married couple, is the way we make decisions. Every decision we ever made ended up with a good outcome. Oh, we had good advice given to us from some key people, but we made good decisions."

Ruth Ann interrupted Ted's heart-felt comments with her own contribution on their success as a couple. She said, "One year Ted went out and did some early Christmas shopping. He came back with his arms loaded with what I thought were gifts. I asked him, "What is all that stuff you are carrying into the house?" He said 'Just some stuff." A few days later, when he was gone from the house, I looked around. I found his stuff. I found a box on the closet shelf that looked interesting. I am sure it was to be wrapped and given as a Christmas gift. I took it down off the shelf and opened it. It was a beautiful, soft, and cushy pair of house shoes. I took them out of the box and tried them on. They were the most comfortable, perfect fitting, snug and cozy house shoes I had ever experienced. I put them on and wore them all day. Every day before Christmas, when Ted was not around, I took them out of the box and wore them all day. When Ted does those kinds of things it makes me really feel good. Those little things are what makes these seventy years so great!"

Of significance, was the comment Joan made as we discussed her dad and mom's relationship. Joan used the word that has been used before, "covenant." She said, "Their relationship was a oneness, solid, it went beyond commitment." For them, their marriage was first. They approached their marriage, their relationship to each other as a work in progress. It was if they had a special saying, "We will work it out."

As I observed their relationship over the years, it goes beyond solid. There is more of a personal touch to describe their bond to each other. That personal touch is characterized as trustful, comfortable, worthy, showing no weakness or uncertainty. They both were recipients of those qualities. Joan added to what fashioned the relationship of her mom and dad, "They had this covenant with each other that had no room for divorce or even indifference."

One of Ruth Ann's closest friends is Nancy Anderson Howell. Nancy spoke of their relationship from her own personal observation. "There was an exclusiveness about their relationship to everyone and everything. That exclusiveness was manifest in the way they looked out for each other. They were always on the same page on issues before them and on decisions to be made." Working together does not define that aspect of "together." It goes much deeper than that. It has to do with the value they place on *being* together. In many cases it is not just a value, but the essence of who they are. *Together* is them.

Ruth Ann made family experiences live on in the life of the family by making sure there was something of a lasting testament to their place in the family's history. How to remember the first Christmas after their marriage? Take the wishbone from the turkey and keep it as a treasured memento.

How to put in place Ted's important years at Millikin as an athlete? Keep in pristine condition, his letter sweater and jacket.

How to put in words the meaning and significance of their relationship? Ted tried to think of a way to make their twentieth anniversary have a touch of meaning and significance. What could he do to express or introduce or surprise Ruth Ann to let her know how he felt? Ted decided he would write something to try to express his feelings. He wrote a poem and it became a treasurer in their relationship and it hangs on the bedroom wall. The note gives the essence of how Ruth Ann made family experiences live on in a very special way in the lives of each one in the Smith family.

Just Twenty Years

Has it been twenty years since we said "I do?

Time sure goes fast when I'm with you.

So many times, together we have said, thought, and done

Only a few days of sadness and twenty years of fun.

First there was Jan and then there was Joan

Two beautiful daughters so we are not alone.

Graduation from College, that was a thrill

Remember the Findlay trip? I know I always will.

The training program, a summer in Columbus with Mrs. Yaw,

But the four of us were together so we had a ball.

Now we are in Terre Haute, corner of 25th and Cruft

The girls are in school and things aren't so tough.

Easters have come and gone, they just won't tarry,

On Easter 9 years ago we got Pepe and Sherri.

More years go by and we are home again,

In 1967 the Two Tony's venture began.

The girls have grown up, and we are getting older,

In some ways we are more conservative and in other ways we
are bolder.

Now we have a place at the lake and work we can share,

Where we can all be together without a single care.

So it's been 20 years since that morning in May,

Well I've enjoyed every minute of it, needless to say.

Jan and Joan echo the same expressions when they talk about their mom and dad's relationship. "It is and always has been easy to see and feel that they love each other. The way they treat each other is so unselfish, thoughtful, and caring. Dad would have an embrace, a pat, a touch, a word of affection and he would just let it flow. They never said a cross word to each other. There was never a moment we questioned their love for each other. Their love for each other was a great testament to us as to what we want our marriages to be. They were the model."

Their friends, Lance and Terri, said they would do things together, just to be together. "If one was to work in the yard, the other would be there. If one was wall papering, the other would help out. When there were people gathered in a home in a social occasion, they would be in the same room together. You never saw them too far away from each other."

The manifestation of that love was found in the four of them as a family. To test the level of that manifestation I asked Jan, what was your finest accomplishment that really pleased your parents? "I think graduation from college and having a career. I think they are pleased that I accomplished so much in my jobs. I believe they are pleased that I am the kind of mother I am. I am sure they are pleased with the kind of young man my son is. I raised a great son, a very good man."

When asked, "Do you remember a time that you disappointed your parents? Joan was very frank and straight forward, "I turned their hair gray. I was independent, strong willed, and different compared to the expectations of a docile 'do as you're told' kind of daughter. But I was never belligerent or never tried to test them. I was what one might describe, my own person."

In spite of the differences that make up their backgrounds and define who they are, Ted and Ruth Ann found a bond that unites them, that guaranteed them spending the rest of their lives with each other as a married couple. It was said by a close family member, that Ted was older by one year and Ruth Ann needed that in her life. She needed an older person whom she could look up to, even if it was only one year older. The issue was, Ted was a mature seventeen-year-old boy.

Ted was the person she could lean on, find stability with. Someone to take her moving in first gear to gear her down to a pace which would allow them to walk with each other, find a presence with each other, and fashion the life they have.

Ruth Ann found in Ted a rock on which to hold on to make her steady. If someone would say there was going to be a reunion of the players of the football team of 1957 and Ted will be going to it, Ruth Ann would tell the organizer of the reunion, "It will be a cold day in hell before he goes to a reunion by himself. I will be the only wife there!"

For the past several generations, it has become too common to hear that in many families there is evidence of that family being dysfunctional. There are many causes for brokenness, lack of fulfillment, lost opportunities, low expectations, and lack of commitment in families. There are also reasons why some families make it, why they are an example of the model family, why they are solid and free of disjointedness.

Ted and Ruth Ann have those characteristics of a loving family locked into their FHA DNA. ("Family's Healthy Attributes as the DNA.") As one considers and looks into several families for a smoking gun, one could not find any "elephants in the room," "dirty laundry," "hidden skeletons," or anything to put a damper on the "chemistry" or "make-up" of Ted and his three girls. Probably the most dominant theme I have heard from Ted is "I can't tell you how proud we are of our girls. They have been such a blessing to us. Their families have enriched our lives, as parents and grandparents, we could not be more happy or more fulfilled."

"There is a long list, a rich litany of accomplishments they have achieved that we take great pride in. They have accomplished so much academically but used that education to be a tool of progress for those they worked with. As educators they have contributed to the development of so many young lives."

A trait that lends authenticity to the quality of their family is defined by the humble spirit of the two girls. They have accomplished a great deal and aspired to so much and have not called attention to themselves. They have raised children and could easily be "bumper-sticker-parents" with the bumper-sticker that says, "MY SON IS THE BEST TENNIS PLAYER IN OKLAHOMA." Or, the bumper-sticker might say, "MY SON IS THE BEST GOLFER IN TEXAS."

The parents do not fashion comments that draw attention to themselves. Nor do they seek to beat their own drums. That is something they learned from their parents. Ted and Ruth Ann were and are such personalities that calling attention to themselves would have been easy. But it didn't happen.

The prophet Micah echoed the same kind of message. Micah said, and it fits a theme that mirrors so much of what Ted and Ruth Ann are about, *"What does God require? What the Lord requires is to do justice, love kindness, and walk humbly with your God. (Micah 6:8)*

The girls never blew their own horns. And there are many accolades for which they could have been recognized. For instance, Ted tells of the time It took a great deal of effort for Joan to speak up at a conference where the question was raised, "Who in our attendance today was ever a beauty queen?" After several hours of scouring the audience, Joan raised her hand and meekly and mildly said, "I was Miss White County." Then, the response was raised as a question, "White?"

Jan had the position of counseling and post-high school advising on schools and employment opportunities. She had the responsibility of working with and guiding over 3,000 high school students to the "next step."

A testament to her notoriety was very evident one day at Two Tony's. Behind the cash register at the "pay-your-bill" counter, were pictures of the girls, Jan and Joan. One person on the way out and while paying his bill, saw the picture of Jan and said, "I know that woman, she was my professor at Eastern Illinois University." Ruth Ann said to him, "She is my daughter."

This has been a narrative on two people, a husband and wife, who began their married life with several strikes against them. But that never stopped them from fashioning their lives together as a model for so many others. The narrative finds its focus, its ending as an affirmation of all the good they instilled in the lives of their girls. So, the question is, "Why did these two girls become the confirmation and culmination of a wonderful love story?" I asked the question to their mom. She answered with an absolute word that spoke volumes of parental pride and love. Ruth Ann simply said, "They are damn good girls."

Nancy Howell added that "The girls were good because Ted and Ruth Ann made sure of that. They attended all the girl's activities to show their support and to let them know of their affirmation of who they are. Ted and Ruth Ann also let them know the boundaries, the limits they could go and do."

To add great meaning, to confirm the rich blessing that Ted and Ruth Ann experience with their family, a special occasion was in order. Of deep significance and put together to send an important message, was the twentieth wedding anniversary of Ted and Ruth Ann. It truly was a family affair! When they got married in 1953, they eloped. They did not have a big wedding that a couple like them would be expected to have. They did not have a big crowd to help them celebrate. They did not have friends to share that most important moment. They did not have a reception with which to make the occasion a grand moment. They did not have a cake to cut. They did not have wedding gifts to open.

For their twentieth anniversary, Ted and Ruth Ann wanted the event to epitomize what their wedding in 1953 should have been. They wanted this celebration to be remembered for a long time. Very few anniversaries are filled with the emotions that define who the couple is or has become. The memories that Ted and Ruth Ann brought to a twenty-year anniversary, are all rich, meaningful, and give a witness to twenty years of overcoming so many strikes against them. The feeling of lost opportunities is no longer waning in the back of their minds. The reality of a true and valued love is confirmed, continued, and made manifest in this beautiful relationship.

After twenty years, Ruth Ann had more work to do and more to say about their girls. As she ate anniversary cake and reveled in the celebration of twenty years, she said, "We wanted to do all we could to make their lives flow in the direction of being hassle-free. We thought of what we might do and planned as much as possible to make their lives less stressful, complicated, and complex. And, it started with their names. A simple name they had....Smith. What can we do to put some emphasis on being unique in spite of having a name like Smith. We made the contribution by using a middle name that would make it less ordinary and more simple. Jan's middle name is Korbet and Joan's middle name is Patrice. That was our first parental decision that was made for, we thought, the good of the girls."

Ted was quick to show me a letter his grandson gave him. He said, "My grandson, Court and his mom Joan, came to visit one time, and Court brought a letter with him that was addressed to "Kakaw," that is his word for me, for grandpa. It was in an envelope and he handed it to me. I opened the envelope and then he comes into the room and sits down. He said, 'you going to read it?' 'Should I?' 'Yea, go ahead.' After I read it I bawled like a baby. I couldn't hold back the tears."

Court was the number one tennis player in the state of Oklahoma. He could have played at Oklahoma University but he said he had enough of tennis. He wrote the following letter to his grandpa about thirty-five years ago. He is married to Megan and they have three children, Sam, Slone, and Scarlet.

Dearest Kakaw,

This letter has been a long time in the making. I have thought to myself many times over the years that I need to take some time and write down how much you have meant to me throughout my life. When my dad passed away last year I decided I needed to stop just thinking about it and make it a priority. There are a number of things that I wish I would have actually told my dad instead of just thinking about it, but it is often hard to stop long enough during a busy day to give time to your thoughts. I didn't want time to get away from me again so here are some thoughts that I have put down in words.

I have always looked up to you so much kakaw. When I was little I always thought of you as this larger than life, superhero-like figure. You were the All-American football playing, horse racing, business owning, king of Carmi in my youthful eyes. I watched your every move and listened to your every word with incredible admiration.

I have such fond memories of coming to stay in Carmi when I was young. It was a highlight of every summer. I was always so proud to parade around Carmi with you and Kinky. Not only did you guys always make me feel like I hung the moon, but it always seemed like everyone else who we came in contact with thought our family hung the moon too! It made me feel special.

I remember going to the barn to jog the horses. I loved getting to do this with you. It was a blast to be around the horses and get to ride with you occasionally. That said, as far as hobbies go, I can't think of many other hobbies that require as much hard work and dedication as training and racing horses. You had a way of making it look easy and fun. I remember getting to go to the coffee shop after we finished with the horses. It was cool that I got to tag along with you everywhere you went. I truly relished every moment I got with you. The hot chocolate was good too!

I remember going to Two Tony's with you in the mornings. You would get me a cinnamon roll while you talked to the employees to make sure that everything was being prepared. I liked walking around with you and pretending to be a boss too. I remember how much respect you demanded from everyone at the restaurant. It was not a forced type of respect, but rather an earned respect. Everyone who worked at Too Tony's knew how hard you and Kinky worked and how fair you were to them and it made them want to be their best too.

I remember going to the Carmi Country Club to play golf. When I look back, I really think that it was during those few summers that I truly learned how to play. I had so much fun playing golf with you and the other guys in the group. You were an excellent teacher too. You were patient and encouraging. At the same time, you would not stand for bad sportsmanship or temper tantrums which I may have been a little prone to. I often let my competitiveness get the best of me!

I remember you leaving your leftover change on the dresser every time I came to your house or when you came to visit us in Oklahoma. It was one of the few things that I could look forward to when we had to part ways and the trip was over. I always thought I was rich when I saw how many quarters you had left behind for me! Memories like these are etched in my mind forever.

You are unlike many others who I have admired when I was young only to see them tumble from the pedestal that I placed them on as I grew older and began to comprehend the traits that make a good man. The more I understood about you the more my admiration grew and that continues today. You are a role model in the truest sense of the word.

You are a great husband. You are so patient with Kinky. Your relationship seems miraculous to someone from my generation. Against the odds at best. You guys got married at such a young age and stayed together through everything that life has thrown at you over the years. It is amazing! It seems like you have always made sure that your marriage was a priority and I strive to do the same with Megan. I admire how great of a husband you are.

You are a great father. I know my mom thinks you are the very best! All the stories that are told about you when my mom was growing up revolve around your unconditional love and support. There was never a doubt about how much you cared for your family. I know I have felt the same love and support as your grandson. I can only hope that in the years to come my family will feel the same about me. I admire how great of a father you are.

Your morals are unwavering. It almost seems like the gray area doesn't exist to you. There is only right and wrong. You are honest, but that word doesn't even seem to do you justice. You ALWAYS choose the path of truth. I have seen you make those choices on numerous occasions. It's not just that you do the right thing, it's that doing the wrong thing is inconceivable to you. You can't even fathom why anyone would choose that path. This truly is one of your greatest qualities and a source of great admiration. I admire your honesty and your morals.

I have learned so much from you and I will continue to draw on that wisdom forever. I think my admiration for you has had to do with the paths I have chosen in my own life. I have always wanted to impress you. I still do.

I love you Kakaw.
Court

Court's mother, Joan, had this to say about how, in this culture that seems so bent on destroying itself, persons can find stability, order, and the strength of abiding love to enrich their lives.

"We live in a culture that (if they marry), it is as though they sign a contract that can be broken, not a covenant that is for life. With a covenant, divorce is not an option, so you work at solutions to a deeper more abiding love that carries the marriage through the difficult times. You create a thriving history together where you know your spouse's personality so well you can adapt to situations like my parents have."

Seventy years of marriage! A wide range of experiences have taken place in the lives of Ted and Ruth Ann in those seventy years. In those seventy years, Jan and Joan, grandkids and great grandkids, extended family, and their close friends have been impacted, molded, and fashioned as to who they are by the love and influence of Ted and Ruth Ann.

How have the past seventy years impacted them? They have had a boat-load of experiences that have fashioned their individual lives and relationship. Their politics, their values and priorities, their religion and how they practice their faith, whether one is conservative or liberal and the place of education in their lives have all been shaped by those seventy years.

In spite of all they have been exposed to and in spite of all they have had to adjust to and work through, they have made it. WWII, the Korean War, the turmoil and unsettledness of Viet Nam, the uncertainties of the decade of the 60's, the counter-revolution atmosphere of the 70's, the tragedies of assassinations, and the many crises of the past seventy years did not have a negative impact on their relationship. Even at the very beginning, with all the strikes against them, with all the insurmountable obstacles facing them, they fulfilled their resolve to be *confident and trustworthy*. They wanted to show their best selves. They wanted to show a level of maturity and responsibility that conveyed *confidence and trust*.

How does one measure a person? How does one measure the lives and relationship of Ted and Ruth Ann? Ruth Ann said it this way, "He stretched me beyond anything I could have accomplished." Ted's response? "What a great life. Thanks to Ruth Ann and the Lord."